IN THE
NATIONAL INTEREST

General Sir John Monash once exhorted a graduating class to 'equip yourself for life, not solely for your own benefit but for the benefit of the whole community'. At the university established in his name, we repeat this statement to our own graduating classes, to acknowledge how important it is that common or public good flows from education.

Universities spread and build on the knowledge they acquire through scholarship in many ways, well beyond the transmission of this learning through education. It is a necessary part of a university's role to debate its findings, not only with other researchers and scholars, but also with the broader community in which it resides.

Publishing for the benefit of society is an important part of a university's commitment to free intellectual inquiry. A university provides civil space for such inquiry by its scholars, as well as for investigations by public intellectuals and expert practitioners.

This series, In the National Interest, embodies Monash University's mission to extend knowledge and encourage informed debate about matters of great significance to Australia's future.

Professor Margaret Gardner AC
President and Vice-Chancellor,
Monash University

SIMON HOLMES à COURT

THE BIG TEAL

MONASH
UNIVERSITY
PUBLISHING

Monash University Publishing
Matheson Library Annexe
40 Exhibition Walk
Monash University
Clayton, Victoria 3800, Australia
https://publishing.monash.edu

Monash University Publishing brings to the world publications which advance the best traditions of humane and enlightened thought.

ISBN: 9781922633569 (paperback)
ISBN: 9781922633583 (ebook)

Series: In the National Interest
Editor: Louise Adler
Project manager & copyeditor: Paul Smitz
Designer: Peter Long
Typesetter: Cannon Typesetting
Proofreader: Gillian Armitage
Printed in Australia by Ligare Book Printers

A catalogue record for this book is available from the National Library of Australia.

THE BIG TEAL

I wasn't there at the beginning. The community independents movement started long before I got involved, built by literally thousands of people. Many have put more blood, sweat and tears into the movement than me but will never receive any public recognition, nor do they seek it.

It's not centrally coordinated, not run from the top. There's no-one to oversee public relations or branding. There's no rule book, no franchisor, no leadership. Most in the media and political class still don't understand it—either because they can only see the world through an outdated two-party frame, or because it suits their purposes to misrepresent it.

Over the eight months between the launch of Kylea Tink's campaign in September 2021 through to the federal election on 21 May 2022, the media struggled to apply a label. More often than not, the movement was overlooked and the focus was on the candidates, devoid of context. Initially they were labelled 'Voices of' candidates, which is, mostly, not actually true—most candidates were entirely independent of local 'Voices of' groups. News Corp and the Liberal Party labelled them 'so-called independents' or 'fake independents', which was insulting but also counterproductive for the accusers. Too often, they were labelled Climate 200 candidates, which they're not, and some even went as far as tagging them 'Simon Holmes à Court's puppets', an ultimately futile attempt to demean and diminish the capable women who had put themselves forward for election.

Just four weeks out from the poll, many in the media settled on a term that became dominant—'the teals'. For some, this refers to the colour the community candidates ran under, although I don't think any adopted teal for their branding but rather orange, coral, blue, green, turquoise, purple, yellow, pink, aqua, navy, peach, olive and burgundy. Others claim that 'teal' refers to a mix of blue and green, representing a blend of centre-right and environmental values—imperfect, but not entirely wrong.

More than a few in the movement are uncomfortable with the teal label, arguing that the grouping erases individual differences; others see no problem with it. As for journalists, a few have explained to me that their job requires a short adjectival phrase and 'community independents' is too much of a mouthful.

A political commentator reminded me that almost all political movements have been strongly associated with a colour—blue for conservatism, green for environmental-ism, grey for senior citizens, purple for feminism, black for anarchism, brown for fascism—and that teal is a perfectly OK colour, unburdened by negative associations. I've asked a few independent MPs what they think. None are fazed by the label, and none felt it was a hill they'd die on. I'd say there's general agreement that it's a fine, if accidental, brand. No doubt I'll upset a few friends in the movement, but for now I'll be using the term 'teal' interchangeably with 'community independent'.

Independents aren't new, but in recent generations they have been rare, with only fourteen elected to the House of Representatives between the end of World War II and 2013. However, in the nine years from the election of Cathy McGowan in 2013, Australians have elected eleven independents to the House, plus two to the Senate. What's new and critically important about the emergence of the teals is that this isn't about political aspirants putting themselves forward, but rather already successful Australians being tapped on the shoulder by their communities.

The community independents—the teals—were the biggest story of the 2022 federal election. They represent arguably the biggest change in Australian politics over the past generation, and they mark a new era in our politics.

This is my perspective on what just happened. I write here about my place, and that of Climate 200, in a vast, decentralised and highly dynamic movement.

AT THE AUBURN

'I'm sorry, I'm going to have to ask you to leave.'

'Sorry, what?'

'The treasurer wants you to leave now.'

'Ummm, okay. Can I just finish my wine first?'

My friend Fiona pleaded, either audibly or with her eyes, I can't remember which, *Please don't make a scene.* She needn't have worried. I'm too much of an introvert. Seconds later I was alone on the footpath, glass of red wine still in my hand, contemplating how strange it all was.

A parent at Fiona's son's school had decided to host a 'meet the candidate' event for Josh Frydenberg just weeks before the May 2019 election, at the Auburn Hotel in Hawthorn East. Fiona had been invited and could bring a 'plus one'. She'd never been to a political meeting but was curious. She also knew I was interested in all things political and asked me if I'd accompany her.

Minutes before I was ushered out of a side door of the hotel, Frydenberg, who was working his way around the room, had greeted me with a firm handshake and a big grin. Hail fellow well met. I'd introduced him to Fiona and then we made small talk about the rigours of campaigning. So after my ejection, my primary emotion was confusion: Why did he throw me out? What did he think I was going to do?

Then it hit me. After six years of cordial acquaintance, Frydenberg was completely shutting me out. If there was a moment when I realised that attempting change from the inside was a fool's errand, at least when it came to this man and this political party, that was it.

Fast-forward three years, to 21 May 2022, and I was back inside the Auburn, standing glass in hand along with 1200 other Kooyong locals, waiting to see whether Monique Ryan, the independent candidate for Frydenberg's seat, would win the night. Around the country, at similar election-night parties, were twenty-two like-minded hopefuls who had sought and received support from Climate 200.

As early as 8 p.m., Antony Green was musing that Mackellar, North Sydney, Wentworth and Goldstein could fall to independents. 'This is more complicated than I expected,' he giggled at one point in the ABC's coverage. At 8.45 p.m., Liberal strategist Tony Barry was calling it a 'teal bath', riffing off the term the media had finally settled on for the people who had sacrificed their professional careers and leaned on their families so as to enter the brutal world of political campaigning.

Mackellar fell first, to Olympic-level athlete and local GP Sophie Scamps, toppling Jason Falinski on Sydney's northern beaches. Wentworth and North Sydney followed soon after, the former to Allegra Spender, a business-woman of 'royal' Liberal blood (her father and grandfather were both Liberal MPs), and the latter to Kylea Tink, the former McGrath Foundation CEO who gave Australian cricket the annual Pink Test.

Then it was Kooyong's turn. When two historically conservative booths reported strong swings towards the challenger, Ryan's campaign director, Ann Capling, let out a squeal of excitement. It was becoming increasingly clear that Frydenberg's hopes of leading the Liberals, if not remaining treasurer, were turning to dust. Everyone present will forever have flashbacks when they hear Whitney Houston's 'I'm Every Woman'.

Next was Goldstein, which like the other seats had been in conservative hands since its inception. Former longtime ABC foreign correspondent Zoe Daniel vanquished Tim Wilson, one-time culture warrior for the Institute of Public Affairs. Last in line were Kate Chaney, also of Liberal heritage—her uncle served in Malcolm Fraser's cabinet, her grandfather in Robert Menzies's—in the blue-ribbon Perth seat of Curtin, and Dai Le, who snatched Fowler in Western Sydney, seeing off Labor frontbencher Kristina Keneally.

The forty-seventh parliament was now home to seven new independent MPs, six of them supported by Climate 200. A former captain of the Wallabies Rugby Union team, David Pocock, also supported by Climate 200, made history by becoming the first independent to represent a territory—the ACT—in the Senate.

It was quite some vindication.

Around the country, more than 20 000 people had volunteered to help the community independent candidates: 2000 in Kooyong alone, and similar numbers in Goldstein and the Australian Capital Territory. For many, it was their first active involvement in an election campaign. They'd been energised by the promise of doing politics differently, and by the sense that the major parties, especially the Coalition, were ignoring if not actively disparaging the issues they most cared about, notably climate change, integrity in politics and gender equity.

Community independents garnered more first-preference votes across twenty-seven seats than Clive

Palmer's United Australia Party (UAP) received across all 151 seats. And did so with about one-fifth of the expenditure, proof that while money matters in politics, people power is more important.

It was vindication, too, for the 11 200 donors to Climate 200 who had put their hands in their pockets to raise more than $13 million to help level the campaign playing field for the community independents.

THE COMMUNITY INDEPENDENT

Climate 200 was an important piece of a wonderfully complex, amorphous and dynamic movement that up-ended traditional, polarised politics in a range of previously safe seats in 2022, but the push for change started almost a decade earlier.

The movement's birthplace was the formerly long-time Liberal seat of Indi in northern Victoria. In 2012, a coalition of frustrated young locals came together with community elders, determined to address the area's 'brain drain'. The area had been neglected by federal government infrastructure programs, and too many of its youths were leaving to live in the cities, many frustrated by the forced choice between home and opportunity. Using organising techniques pioneered by the Victorian Women's Trust under Mary Crooks, the group built a non-partisan political movement focused on identifying shared values and awakening the community to the possibility of genuine representation.

The group chose Cathy McGowan to run against incumbent Liberal MP Sophie Mirabella, who had told agitators that 'the people of Indi aren't interested in politics'.[1] On election day, more than 500 locals wore orange T-shirts to show their allegiance to the community independent, and after eleven days of counting McGowan was declared the winner by just 439 votes. The people of Indi had proven that a major party MP who neglected to listen could be toppled by a meticulously organised community campaign. McGowan's subsequent record in parliament, winning infrastructure and other improvements for Indi, notably telecommunications and transport, would turn her narrow victory in 2013 into a solid majority in 2016.

In 2018, Kerryn Phelps seized the seat of Wentworth in Sydney's eastern suburbs from the Liberals after Malcolm Turnbull's political decapitation and subsequent resignation forced a by-election. Phelps's victory proved that the bluest of blue-ribbon seats could be won by a strong community campaign. She advocated an end to Australia's disgraceful treatment of asylum seekers in offshore detention, which in turn led to the successful introduction of the Medevac legislation—albeit the success was short-lived.

At the 2019 federal election, Indi achieved another first. McGowan had decided to retire, but the community infrastructure she had nurtured and her record in parliament enabled her successor candidate, Helen Haines, to retain the seat—the first time an independent had managed to assist a like-minded hopeful to do so.

At the same election, former barrister and Olympian Zali Steggall took on former prime minister Tony Abbott in a David-and-Goliath battle in Warringah on Sydney's North Shore. Steggall's victory provided further proof that the community independent model could be just as potent in a high-income urban electorate as it had been in a lower-income rural area. Meanwhile, Rebekha Sharkie, who first won the seat of Mayo in the Adelaide Hills as a member of the Nick Xenophon Team in 2016, had developed her own style as a fiercely independent advocate for an area that had 'belonged' to the Liberal Party for generations.

Climate 200, established just six weeks before the 2019 election, provided support to Haines's and Sharkie's victories as well as nine unsuccessful independent campaigns, including those run by Kerryn Phelps and Julia Banks. Had just three of the nine won, this book may have been written three years earlier, but the wave was not there—we weren't ready for it.

The 2019 federal election was a great disappointment to the many who hoped it would be a 'climate election'. Like the dog that catches the car, the Coalition didn't know what to do when Scott Morrison's 'miracle' unexpectedly returned it to office. Labor, meanwhile, retreated from an expansive and courageous policy offering into the political equivalent of PTSD. Morrison's government soon became synonymous with mismanagement and corruption. This, coupled with the small-target strategy Labor adopted to win back government, made the forty-sixth parliament a dark and uninspiring place. But against this background, the independents—Steggall, Haines, Sharkie, and veteran Tasmanian independent Andrew Wilkie—shone.

Over the previous decade, independents had demonstrated that high-integrity, focused individuals could make a difference, impacting the national political discussion and winning locals' affection. In particular, Steggall's Climate Change Bill was in line with the concerns of her community and many others. The failure of self-styled 'Modern Liberals' like Trent Zimmerman to support the bill, and the refusal of the Morrison government even to allow it to be debated, struck a chord with voters in a range of electorates beyond Warringah.

Steggall's promotion of her legislation put climate change on the 2022 election agenda in a way none of the major parties wanted. The Coalition and Labor had both shied away from meaningful engagement on climate like Dracula from a stake, an omission not missed by voters in electorates around the country. (Although it was never the intention, and Labor might never acknowledge it, by forcing the Coalition to fight on two fronts—climate denial in some areas, net zero by 2050 in others—and doubling the number of battleground seats, the independents assisted Anthony Albanese to a majority.)

Equally, Haines's promotion of a national anti-corruption commission highlighted Morrison's breach of the promise made during the last campaign. So, too, Morrison's highly criticised response to serious allegations of sexual harassment, and worse, inflicted on the female staff of MPs and senators.

Climate, integrity and women's safety added up to a bundle of concerns that resonated in electorates across the nation. But Morrison, his government and his MPs—despite what had already happened in Indi, Mayo and Warringah—thought it safe to ignore these concerns, believing they could be dismissed because, as one conservative commentator put it, those seats 'rightfully belonged' to the Coalition.

They were about to be proved wrong.

BUSINESS AND CONSCIENCE

My father was an enigma, and I think he liked it that way. It's fitting that the sculpture memorialising him on the family farm carries the Lord Byron quote: 'I stood among them, but not of them—in a shroud of thoughts which were not their thoughts.'

He was often a little overdressed. His accent was hard to place, having grown up in Zimbabwe (then Rhodesia) in a family that considered itself British, then being sent to boarding school in South Africa. He spoke slowly, deliberately, confidently, with long, uncomfortable pauses. He left Africa when he was nineteen and, for reasons no-one has ever been able to explain, started a degree in forestry at Massey University in New Zealand. It says a lot about him that no-one is sure exactly what he did between 1956 and 1962, when he moved to Perth and enrolled as a mature-age law student at the University of Western Australia.

The only personal history he passed down of his upbringing was a handful of stories from his school days: pranks (unhitching train carriages, snakes placed in a teacher's bed), early businesses (a taxi service, school photography) and hardships (a morning dip in a freezing plunge pool in lieu of showers). He never mentioned his father, who died long before I was born, and while he made sure his own mother's needs were always taken care of—by delegating them to my mother—I never saw him express any affection towards her.

He was a workaholic, not stopping for weekends or public holidays. When staff told him they were having trouble keeping up, he suggested they 'sleep faster'. He spent most of each day seated either thinking in silence or on the phone, smoking Henri Wintermans Long Panatella cigars—thirty or even forty a day was not unusual—and playing computer chess. Even when he was attempting a takeover of BHP, Australia's then largest company, if we asked him what he'd done that day, he'd say, 'Fiddled about.'

While he had many strong relationships within his work, he invested no time in a social life, which left him with almost no friends, a fact that likely never occurred to him. He did have a strong bond with Eugene Halstead, the husband of a woman he had taxied from Zimbabwe to South Africa in his school days. The family had lost three of its members in the Zimbabwean war of independence, and my father worked hard to get them out of Africa and into a new life in Australia. He was also close to Charles Bright, ostensibly his stockbroker, but their almost daily, hour-long chats were mainly about philosophy.

He had high expectations of his four children, once giving me what I now consider terrible advice: 'You can be whatever you want to be, but be the best in the world.' Like many of his generation, he wasn't the type to hug his children or tell them he loved them, but periodically he took the time to teach a skill—swimming, boxing, futures trading. The flashes of understated approval we received when we'd done something well gave us the best feeling in the world.

For as long as I knew him, he never went shopping for food or clothes, visited a hairdresser (they came to him), cooked a meal or packed a suitcase. From the moment she quit her job as a science teacher, having satisfied her Education Department scholarship teaching commitment, and went to work in my father's legal practice, right up until the end of his life, my mother Janet freed my father from the thousands of little tasks that normal folk do as a matter of course. She freed him to think and do.

Mum was busy. Not only did she insulate my father from all domestic duties, she had four kids, and while we were young she sat on the boards of the Cancer Council WA, Diabetes Research Foundation, Save the Children Fund, Australian Children's Television Foundation and a dozen other charities. She had help on the home front but did most of the cooking and shopping herself, until, at the peak of my father's career, the family convinced her this was unsustainable and she reluctantly capitulated.

Michael Robert Hamilton Holmes à Court, known by his middle name Robert, was a spectacularly successful businessman, building an eclectic empire of assets that included newspapers, television, mining equipment, media rights (including The Beatles, Muppets, Thunderbirds and Nat King Cole), cattle, wine, theatres and property. He made a series of audacious takeover bids for companies many times larger than the one he controlled, Bell Group, and with each attempt he carefully constructed a position whereby he'd profit regardless of whether the bid succeeded or he was forced to retreat. He had no reverence for the Establishment, and he didn't suffer fools.

His empire was rocked by the Black Monday stock market crash of 19 October 1987, which slashed the value of his assets against a very significant debt portfolio. Over the next two years he began a careful restructuring and de-risking of the business, exiting the world of the listed public company. While those close to him saw the toll this was taking, he ignored the many warning signs that his health was failing.

Very early on the morning of Father's Day 1990, he died suddenly of a massive heart attack at the family farm an hour south of Perth, leaving behind a still complex and highly leveraged business. My mother and older siblings were in the room when his heart stopped. My younger brother was on the other side of the country, in his final year of boarding. I was up in Perth at a friend's wild eighteenth birthday. My final conversation with my father took place a few days prior, actually an argument, never to be resolved. Frustrated about something or other, he had unloaded on my mother. I told him he had no right to 'treat her like shit'. We'd never spoken like that before.

After he died, my mother was inundated with unsolicited advice, mostly recommending that she sell up and go sit on a beach. That was never going to happen. Audaciously, she took over the business—the Heytesbury group—and, over a tough decade, reshaped it to her personality. While my father had raided and traded assets, my mother was more interested in what she'd call 'doing things'. She sold assets that weren't productive, fortified the beef, wine and theatre businesses, and acquired others like John Holland Constructions, which had built Australia's new Parliament House and the MCG's Great Southern Stand. To this day, hardly a week goes by without a stranger telling me they met her ten, twenty, thirty years ago and were touched by her genuine interest in them.

My earliest memories of my mother are of her planting trees. Getting her hands dirty, she worked with teams to plant tens of thousands of trees on our family farm, located an hour south of Perth on the Darling Scarp, abutting the jarrah forests that are increasingly being downed for bauxite mining. She'd say that Dad did the horses and she did the trees. Dad loved the way that trees transformed both the microclimate and the aesthetics of

SIMON HOLMES À COURT

the place, protecting his horses and making it feel more
like an estate than a dry farm.

Every other year, during school holidays, Mum took us
kids down to the south-west of Western Australia, where
the majestic karri trees create forests of outstanding beauty.
She would show us the trees, then take us 100 metres back
from the road to witness the denuded landscape left by
clear-felling. I remember a deep sense of loss and outrage
at the loggers' deceit—most passers-by would have no idea
that the loggers were hollowing out our forests, extracting
private profits while destroying a public asset.

While it's easy to stereotype my father as the ruthless
businessman and my mother as the social conscience,
there was a significant crossover. While my mother would
obsess about turning off lights to save the planet, and
money, my father recognised that running lower stocking
rates on cattle properties would be good for both the land
and business. My father was immensely proud of Telethon,
the Perth charity he turbocharged to raise millions each
year for profoundly disabled kids, and my mother was
recognised for her business skills, becoming the first
woman to serve on the Reserve Bank of Australia board,
and pro-chancellor of the University of Western Australia.

Oddly, throughout my journey with Climate 200,
pretty much every article written on the subject has chosen
to portray me as a son of Australia's first billionaire, even
though my father has now been dead for thirty-two years.
My mother, whose impressive career spans six decades,
almost never cracks a mention.

I was the odd one out of the four kids: while they were extroverted and outdoors types, I was an introverted nerd. From very early on I had a fascination with energy, infrastructure and computers. At age two and a half I stuck a key into a power point, burning the skin of my index finger and earning me a couple of skin grafts. At age four, I stopped my mother as we were walking through a department store to show her a power point mounted on the floor rather than on the wall: 'Mum! Look at that fantastic power point!' At age five, all I wanted for my birthday was a bag of cement. (My mother did eventually give me one, but not until my eighteenth birthday.)

At age ten, I bought my own computer with money I'd earned from packing fishhooks and lead sinkers on a holiday job. I then painted fences on the family farm to earn enough to upgrade to a newer, faster computer, and at age twelve I bought a modem that allowed me to connect my computer to bulletin board systems (BBS), the precursor to the internet. I wrote computer programs that let me transfer data from one computer to another, my own simple network. My father became a lot more interested in what I was doing when he realised I could access stock prices faster than his stockbroker could fax them.

Several years later, I started my own BBS and networked it to others in the 'eastern states'—the name for everywhere in Australia that's not in WA. It felt incredible to connect to the world outside parochial Perth. Occasionally, I'd dial in to BBS in the United States to download the latest files for sharing on my own network, at great expense to my parents, although amounting to only a tiny fraction of what my father racked up calling business associates around the world for hours at a time.

For as long as I can remember, I've had an engineering mindset. I'm not at peace with a new gadget or technology until I know how it works, and if something's not working it's an immense pleasure to design a solution. It's no mystery to me why I've never been far from the intersection of business, technology, the environment and the non-profit sector.

When my father died, my mother and siblings and I all became business partners. In 2008, we decided to disentangle our business interests. My mantra is that families are a drag on businesses, and businesses are a drag on families—though I believe that some families do manage to make it work.

THE COLDEST PLACE

I started boarding school at age eleven. Geelong Grammar was a four-hour flight from home in Perth, and one of the coldest places in Australia, physically and emotionally.

My parents travelled often and for long periods, and my father believed that, as boarding school had been good for him, it would be good for us kids, too. 'Character building,' he said. The co-ed Geelong Grammar, nestled between a large oil refinery and the rotting seaweed of Limeburners Lagoon, had been recommended by my father's stockbroker friend. One of the more 'English' schools in Australia, I bet it reminded him of his boarding school in South Africa. My two older siblings were already at the school, though such was the stratification that I didn't see my older brother there until my second year, even though his dormitory was only 200 metres from mine.

The school has no doubt changed considerably in the last three decades, but, as highlighted by the Royal Commission into Institutional Responses to Child Sexual Abuse, in the 1980s it was, for many, a hellhole. Physical, psychological and sexual abuse were rife.[2] A friend of mine was forced down a stormwater drain and urinated on by half a dozen boys. As the cooling piss, foul smell and claustrophobia all competed to be the dominant sensation, the boys standing on the grate cheered, amplifying the humiliation. My friend, finally fed up with all the abuse, took his story and an actual dossier of case reports (including witness signatures) to the headmaster. The dossier disappeared, no serious punishment was meted out, and the abuse continued. Character building?

One night a boy had me kneel down on all fours with my chin on a chair. As he whipped my bare legs with a bicycle inner tube, he made the rules clear to me: I would be free to go as soon as I could take a lash without grimacing. At the end of the year he was appointed house captain. Years later I bumped into him at a restaurant in Melbourne and asked him why he'd abused me. He said it was because I was 'self-righteous'.

I probably received the 'average' physical mistreatment and was lucky to avoid the sexual abuse that was prevalent at the time, but there was a group of older boys who despised me for no other reason than my father was successful. Some were the biggest fish in their country-town pond, others were sons of the Melbourne Establishment, but the mere presence of the Holmes à Court boys at the school, and the frequent appearance of our father on the front pages of the papers in the common room, seemed to offend them. (My sister had a different experience. As an accomplished multi-sport athlete and extrovert, she fitted in well with the 'sportocracy'.)

Spending your formative years stuck between fight and freeze modes—flight wasn't an option—numbs the emotions. On the plus side, unless you are the top dog, you become hypersensitive to injustice. And if it doesn't break you, it does make you resilient. Character building!

In the lead-up to the 2022 election, I'd often be asked how I was handling being 'attacked' most nights on Sky After Dark, which refers to the programming on Sky News Australia after the day-shift journalists leave and the reactionary, post-truth opinionistas take over. I'd honestly quip that Sky After Dark was nothing compared with Geelong Grammar After Dark.

GALE AND GUSTO

In 2004, a wind farm developer held a community forum for the proposed Clarkes Hill project in the small town of Dean (pop. 120) in central Victoria. A car full of Daylesford residents drove the 25 kilometres there, excited that a wind farm would be coming to the area. They thought they were walking into an information session, but what transpired was described by one as 'more like a lynching'. The developer was met by an angry mob with a strong message: there'd be nothing but trouble if the project went ahead. If the proposal didn't die on that night, it was certainly mortally wounded.

But something else was born. On the drive home, the Daylesford group shared their disappointment that the first response from 'the community' to wind energy had been reflexive opposition. One of the passengers, Per Bernard, decided he was going to change that. Per, a local builder, is a Dane. He'd seen small municipalities, farmers and community cooperatives take advantage of 1970s energy-crisis tax incentives, such that the majority of Denmark's wind farms were citizen-owned. Danish wind farms enjoy broad and deep community support. Per was enchanted by the cooperative model and decided that was the way to go.

My wife Katrina and I had had a farm in the area for almost a decade. I bumped into Per's makeshift stall on Daylesford's main street one Saturday morning and he explained how a two-turbine wind farm would generate as much electricity annually as the houses in the local area consumed. I signed up as a supporter on the spot.

Every large wind developer in Melbourne had rejected Per's idea as too small, too strange. None had faith that a community could muster the required sophistication or capital. But Per persevered and momentum for the project grew. A town hall meeting was called where it was resolved to form the Hepburn Community Wind Park Co-operative. I went in as an interested supporter and accidentally came out as chairman.

In July 2008 we launched our public offer in Daylesford, hoping to raise $3 million from the community over twelve weeks. For many, it was an idea whose time had come—hundreds quickly signed up. Then the global financial crisis hit and subscriptions stopped as everyone sat on their wallets. Institutional fund managers told us we didn't have a hope in hell of meeting their investment criteria—too small, no track record, too risky—and our bank advised us that instead of 50 per cent debt, we'd be lucky to get half that. The Australian dollar fell sharply, increasing the project's cost—instead of $3 million, we'd need to raise $10 million. And while our project was overwhelmingly supported by the community, the anti-wind wingnuts wanted it dead.

I went into Christmas 2008 feeling devastated. The gulf between where we were and where we needed to be seemed impossibly wide. I felt I was carrying the hopes and dreams of hundreds of investors and thousands of wellwishers, and I felt responsible for delivering an impossible task. I had an inkling of what my father must have felt during the stock market crash twenty-one years earlier and it nearly crushed me. I couldn't see a pathway ahead, but nor did I believe that retreat was an option.

I would not have made it through that period without Katrina's patient understanding and sage advice. I started to accept that I wasn't responsible for how the goalposts kept moving, and that unwinding the project was actually achievable. Thankfully, we were in a position to return every cent we'd raised. As I decoupled my self-worth from the project and accepted that an elegant dismount was at least a possibility, the fog started to lift.

Then a friend, Natalie Toohey, a parent at my kids' school and a crisis communications specialist, took me out for coffee and told me the project was important, worth saving, and she wanted to help. She said the secret was the 'smell of success' and confidence. After she helped us to develop a communications strategy, we went back to everyone who had invested and gave them two choices: withdraw your subscription now and receive a complete refund, or stick with us until we've either raised the money or decided it's impossible, risking some capital. Amazingly, less than 2 per cent of the funds were withdrawn.

With our patient, recommitted investors onboard, we projected new confidence and money started trickling in. 'Success begets success,' as the saying goes—the trickle became a stream. Towards the end, investors were rushing in, worried that they might miss out. Ultimately, it took almost two years to raise all the funds required and sign the construction contracts to build the wind farm. On 19 April 2011, 300 supporters sat in deckchairs and on picnic blankets on Leonards Hill, 10 kilometres south of Daylesford, to witness a giant crane lift the first turbine of Australia's first community-owned wind farm into place. Two months later, a pair of turbines—named Gale and Gusto by a local schoolgirl—fed their clean energy into the grid for the first time.

Hepburn Wind put me at the juncture of community and climate action, engineering and politics. In 2011, the project won the Victorian Premier's Sustainability Award; then premier Ted Baillieu, who famously hated wind farms, left before the award was presented. Hepburn Wind went on to win the World Wind Energy Award for project of the year and evolves to this day, recently changing its name to Hepburn Energy as it prepares to add solar panels and a big battery.

FRYDENBERG

I first met Josh Frydenberg at a Lighter Footprints climate forum in August 2011. Matthew Wright, director of Beyond Zero Emissions, was setting out a future for 100 per cent renewables by the end of the decade. Lane Crocket, general manager of Pacific Hydro, explained the recently upgraded Renewable Energy Target (RET) and how the sector was likely to develop under the settings at the time (large-scale solar then cost $300 per megawatt-hour, more than six times the cost today). Josh Frydenberg was the last speaker.

The member for Kooyong had only been elected a year earlier and used his ten minutes to highlight what he perceived as the shortcomings of renewables and spruik the virtues of nuclear energy. I didn't know much about nuclear at the time, but I knew plenty about renewable energy and believed he had uncritically swallowed someone else's talking points. I introduced myself to him afterwards and suggested we should catch up sometime. It would finally happen almost two years later.

In June 2013, with Tony Abbott as leader, the Liberal Party was signalling that it was backing away from sixteen years of bipartisan support for the RET introduced by John Howard. When Kevin Rudd had increased the RET three years earlier from a nominal 9 per cent by 2010 to 20 per cent by 2020, the Liberals under Turnbull had offered full-throated support. Shadow minister for climate change Greg Hunt had even admonished Rudd for taking so long to increase the target. But now Hunt, a supporter of carbon pricing under Turnbull, had become strongly opposed to it under Abbott.

I arranged a meeting with Frydenberg in his office, where I implored him not to turn out like Hunt, not to burn all credibility with the clean energy and environment sectors. Abbott had relied on Hunt to tear down Julia Gillard's carbon price and to put together Direct Action, the fig-leaf policy that would serve to give the Coalition government cover for not having a credible plan to reduce emissions. I remember saying it was a shame to see a relatively young politician acting, in my view, for short-term political gain, placing himself on the wrong side of history.

Katrina had suggested I take a bottle of wine to the meeting, an offering to demonstrate I had come in good faith and valued Frydenberg's time. And so I began a tradition, bringing along a bottle of Vasse Felix from the Margaret River winery that's been in my family since the late 1980s.

When the conversation was finished, I took the short drive back home. As I pulled into my driveway on that cold June evening, a call from an unknown number came up on my phone. I rarely answer calls from private numbers, but I impulsively took this one. It was Greg Hunt. In the fifteen or so minutes since I'd left Frydenberg's office, the member for Kooyong had called and briefed Hunt, who was incensed by my characterisation of him. And so I joined the very long list of people who have endured one of Hunt's expletive-laden tantrums down a phone line. He was livid that I hadn't laid out my issues with him when I'd attended his office as part of a delegation some two weeks earlier. He shouted on and on about how he was the environment movement's only friend in the Coalition, and yet nothing he ever did was good enough for them.

In my political naivety, I had been unaware that Hunt and Frydenberg were best friends. I later learned through media reports that Hunt had lured Frydenberg into politics, also that Frydenberg was best man at Hunt's wedding, while Hunt was a groomsman at Frydenberg's. The common ground would not stop there—while Hunt entered parliament in 2001, a full nine years before Frydenberg, both men's political careers would end with the forty-sixth parliament.

Despite that experience, I continued to meet with Frydenberg at least annually. Our discussions were convivial—we both enjoyed the chats and the sparring. He was always cautious in his choice of words, always had an adviser present busily scratching down notes. One of my aims was to see if I could help him become a champion within his party on climate policy, but I also wanted to understand him, to know what made the man tick. I remember once telling Frydenberg that climate and energy policy were my strongest passions. He responded that it was 'not really an area of interest' for him. Not long after, he was made minister for the environment and energy.

It was while he still held that portfolio, in 2017, that I joined Kooyong 200, a Liberal Party fundraising body that provided a fighting fund to the then local member. The body is secretive and hugely successful, having raised $4.5 million over the decade to 2021. Being an unincorporated association, its public reporting obligations are only a short form filed annually with the Australian Electoral Commission (AEC); since 2016, not a single donor has been named. The funds collected were not just for the re-election of the Liberal member for Kooyong—perhaps as little as $200 000 was needed to fight each of Frydenberg's first three elections, in 2010, 2013 and 2016. They also gave the up-and-coming MP the power to hand out grants around the party, essential for building the intricate web of obligations that would be so important in the event Frydenberg eventually faced a ballot in the party room for the top job.

In joining Kooyong 200, I wanted to demonstrate to Frydenberg that I was serious about helping him advance in the party, that I supported him.

UNFORCED ERRORS

In March 2018, Josh Frydenberg foolishly picked a fight with AGL, the country's biggest electricity retailer. AGL had bought two ageing coal generators from the NSW Government in 2014 and valued one of them, Liddell, at nothing given its age and condition. The company had already told the market it intended to close Liddell in 2022. Frydenberg was determined to turn that decision around and tried to force AGL to sell the power station to a competitor. When CEO Andy Vesey refused, Frydenberg took the extraordinary and outrageous step of calling members of AGL's board—the board of a publicly listed company!—to pressure them to overrule Vesey.[3]

For five years, I had been following the technical and economic aspects of the closures of thirteen coal-powered stations, and commenting on the federal government's ham-fisted interventions into the electricity sector, which it ramped up after the South Australian blackout in September 2016. In early April 2018, a ginger group called the Monash Forum was established to try to prop up support for coal, and *The Guardian* asked me to write an article to explain what was going on. I was in China on a renewable energy study tour, from where I duly sent off an article titled 'Why Liddell Is Likely to Close in 2022, and Why You Shouldn't Care'.[4] In it, I was gently critical of Josh Frydenberg:

> Lastly, Frydenberg, by all accounts a fine tennis player, has made two unforced errors. As a politician, he should know that narratives matter. Australia's largest carbon emitter, AGL, is spending big advertising that they're getting out of coal—before 2050. AGL's pushback on the government amplifies AGL's positive message a hundredfold and drowns out those disappointed with the slow pace.
>
> The second error, and I concede that I'm speculating, is that Frydenberg might be messing with the wrong guy. AGL's American boss, Andy Vesey, hasn't put down roots in Australia. The time will probably come when he returns to the US. What narrative will he want to take to his next role? That when confronted by bullies, he blinked?

History shows Vesey didn't blink. He did return to the United States, and AGL closed one of Liddell's four units in March 2022, with the remainder to be shuttered in 2023.

As for Frydenberg, he was evidently unimpressed by my piece. Less than twenty-four hours after publication, the Kooyong 200 Club Committee emailed me to say that my membership application had been rejected. Odd phrasing, given that my membership had been accepted a year earlier, and I'd already been invoiced for and paid my second year of dues. Sure enough, two years of membership fees and a donation I'd made were refunded to my credit card.

As 2018 progressed, it was clear that Frydenberg was betting everything on his National Energy Guarantee (NEG), which I strongly opposed. The NEG had two arms. The reliability guarantee was based on the false premise that our grid was unreliable and on the verge of collapse. The emissions guarantee was a convoluted proxy for a carbon price with a target set well below 'business as usual'. I spent two months trying to meet Frydenberg to discuss my concerns before he finally granted me a meeting, in May.

It was a friendly, even lighthearted discussion. I recall Frydenberg's amused smirk when I predicted the NEG would never be legislated. A hundred days later, Turnbull abandoned it after a backbench cabal he likened to terrorists threatened to blow up his government, which they did anyway. However, what really sticks in my mind is that when I brought up the subject of my expulsion from Kooyong 200, Frydenberg initially claimed it wasn't a matter for him but the committee. When I said it was preposterous to claim that the committee booted me without his direction, he decided to engage on the topic. Kooyong 200, he told me, was a place for 'unconditional supporters'. Apparently I ran hot and cold.

The claim struck me: I've never had a professional relationship where loyalty trumped reasoned opinion, or where honest feedback was utterly unwelcome.

My suspicion that the Liberal Party was beyond hope was strongly reinforced.

TWEETS AND TWITS

In early 2017, my then business partner and I sold our fourteen-year-old startup agricultural water-management business. Part of the terms of the sale were that I stay out of the industry for seven years. So I started casting about for what to do next. I dabbled in coding, learning a new programming language, contributing to an open-source home automation project, and deepening the knowledge of renewable energy and climate change I'd gained during my Hepburn Wind days.

One quiet Saturday afternoon in June, I logged on to Twitter and created an account to share my discoveries and insights on Australia's energy transition. I was annoyed by how most of what I read in the media was simply wrong, either based old data or deeply tainted with ideological biases. I found that Twitter was a great place to consult experts, debunk false claims and correct the record.

Chris Kenny, the *Australian* and *Sky News* culture warrior, became one of my first sparring partners. Chris seemed to see me as a 'class traitor', someone who should reflexively support his own flawed arguments simply because of my privilege. He would write a factually incorrect commentary piece about energy and I would quickly follow it up with a fact check. Kenny never challenged my facts, just threw weak ad-hominem barbs in my direction, albeit never scoring a direct hit. Kenny once claimed that my father would have been ashamed of me. To the contrary, my father would have been proud. He had no time for the Establishment, or the men and women who did its bidding in exchange for the crumbs that fell off the table. My father admired courage, intellectual honesty and hard work. He held small men like Kenny in contempt.

I guess Kenny found me annoying. He hurled abuse at me, blocked me, unblocked me, abused me some more, and blocked me again. And at each step, he drew attention to me and my expertise and boosted my profile on the platform. Similarly, I engaged respectfully but persistently with journalists and politicians who, in my opinion, spread misinformation about renewable energy and climate change. It seemed that Twitter liked what I had to say, and over time I became a trusted voice. My following grew organically over the next two years, to the point where my account was routinely in the top ten globally in SustMeme's ranking of 'positive influencers' in the climate and energy category. This gave me a large audience that would prove critical to my involvement in two major campaigns.

The more fragile souls in the media and politics liken Twitter to a sewer, focusing on the antisocial behaviour that occurs on the platform. It can be brutal, and there are people who, protected by anonymity, make rude and abusive comments they'd never say to someone's face. That said, I've found if you block everyone who is clearly not engaging in good faith, it can be an amazing space. Apart from the breaking news, and hilarious and cutting takes on every issue under the sun, the best thing about Twitter is the access to experts, politicians, journalists and opinion shapers. If you've proven you have valuable things to say, you can influence the discussion on Twitter and see it filter through the national media over subsequent weeks.

In October 2018, Alan Jones used his bully pulpit to force the Sydney Opera House to advertise a horse race. Sydneysiders were outraged by how the radio shock jock bullied first the venue's CEO and then the NSW premier into projecting the barrier draw of the $13 million race onto the iconic sails of the World Heritage–listed site, contravening guidelines prohibiting commercial advertising. Then prime minister Scott Morrison, wary of Jones's power, said he couldn't see what the fuss was about: 'It's the biggest billboard in the country.'

Around the same time, a group of refugee advocacy organisations developed the simple but very effective campaign #KidsOffNauru. While Australians experienced a range of emotions about asylum seekers rotting in indefinite offshore detention that prevented resolution of the issue, few were aware that more than 200 kids were growing up in these appalling conditions. Children as young as ten had attempted suicide, and there were many documented reports of sexual assault.

Though unrelated, the atrocities being committed against children in our care on Nauru and Jones's clear abuse of his power triggered my lifelong hatred of bullying and abuse, and a random connection was formed. I was overseas, and in the seconds of wi-fi I had before hopping on a train, I fired off a cheeky tweet:

Oct 7, 2018
hey @SydOperaHouse, i'd like to take out an ad on the opera house sails—a video projection of kids detained on #nauru, one of our national pastimes. i'm willing to pay the same as @NSW_Racing. serious offer—who do i speak with?

When I came back into range a few hours later, I discovered that the tweet had blown up, receiving an order of magnitude more 'likes' than anything I'd ever written before.

A direct message from Prashan Paramanathan of the crowdfunding site chuffed.org was intriguing. When I called him, Prashan answered with 'Welcome to the campaign!' He made the case that my pithy tweet had connected the rage against Alan Jones with the rage against state-sanctioned child abuse, and in doing so I had created a fundraising 'moment' that could really help the #KidsOffNauru campaign. Prashan convinced me to start a crowdfunding campaign. My pitch was simple: help me fund the projection of #KidsOffNauru onto the Opera House, and if the Opera House refuses, I'll spend every cent raised on getting the children off Nauru. Within seventy-two hours, the crowdfunder raised $117000 from more than 1700 donors. The answer from the Opera House, however, was a big fat 'No!' My requests to have the decision reviewed were rebuffed with Kafkaesque efficiency by the offices of the NSW premier and arts minister.

At this point I experienced a twinge of anxiety. I felt the weight of others' hopes and expectations, and—not for the first or last time—an almost crushing responsibility to faithfully spend other people's money. Thankfully, I had access to a brains trust who wanted the best for my project and would help me spend every last cent raised, and a bit more, to get the maximum impact for donors' funds. We rented a video billboard truck and loaded it with the iconic image that we'd planned to project onto the Opera House. A photographer followed the truck around for a day, snapping it at the Opera House, Sydney Harbour Bridge, Bondi Beach and other Sydney landmarks. We paid for buses to help advocates from Melbourne and Sydney attend a rally on the steps of Parliament House, and commissioned Van Thanh Rudd to paint a mural in Melbourne bringing attention to Qantas's participation in the forced deportation of asylum seekers back to the dangers they'd fled.

It was exhilarating to contribute to such a decentralised but effective movement, especially one that was winning. As the pressure increased on the government, the number of children on Nauru began to fall: below 200, down to 150, below 100, into the dozens, and then … none.

Julia Banks's speech to the House of Representatives on 27 November 2018 was a turning point. Elected as the

Liberal member for Chisholm, Banks chose to leave the party after witnessing and being subjected to abysmal treatment in the putsch that rolled Turnbull and installed Morrison. Her decision to move to the crossbench meant that the government lost its majority on the floor of the House of Representatives. I saw how an independent, a crossbencher, free from the ideology of government or the cowed Opposition, could speak the truth on offshore detention. I saw how the crossbench could operate as both the conscience and the backbone of parliament.

The #KidsOffNauru organisers shifted their momentum to a campaign for Medevac. A large number of refugees had been denied medical attention; some had died. The newly elected Kerryn Phelps worked with independent senator Tim Storer to introduce a bill taking the decision for medical evacuations out of the hands of bureaucrats and putting it into the hands of medical professionals. I contacted Phelps and asked how I could help, armed with the remnants of my crowdfunder. We settled on placing a full-page ad in *The Australian* on the day of the vote, and I was privileged to be in the public gallery on 12 February 2019 when the bill was passed—the first time the government had lost a vote on legislation on the floor of parliament in ninety years. The government had opposed the reform—cruelty was integral to their asylum seeker policy—and the Opposition had lacked the backbone to initiate it. Only the crossbench could drive it.

Barely five months later, the Coalition, armed with a slim post-election majority in the House, voted to repeal the Medevac legislation. A trio of medical doctors—Katie Allen, Fiona Martin, David Gillespie—and every other so-called 'moderate' Liberal voted to remove doctors' ability to obtain the necessary medical attention for critically ill detainees held offshore.

CALL ME TRIMTAB

In early 2000 I saw a play that changed my life, called *R. Buckminster Fuller: The History (and Mystery) of the Universe*. Buckminster Fuller was an intellectual giant of the mid-twentieth century, one of the first to discuss the need for a circular economy and best known for inventing the geodesic dome, an icon of mid-twentieth-century futuristic design. Bucky, as he was known, dedicated his life to working on the big problems faced by humanity.

Bucky had a particular fascination with the trimtab, a tiny point in a system where the minimum effort causes the maximum effect, as he explained in a February 1972 *Playboy* interview:

Think of the *Queen Elizabeth* [a transatlantic liner almost twice the size of the *Titanic*]. The whole ship goes by, and then comes the rudder. And there's a tiny thing at the edge of the rudder called a trimtab. It's a miniature rudder. Just moving the little trimtab builds a low pressure that pulls the rudder around. Takes almost no effort at all.

Bucky went on to point out that 'the little individual can be a trimtab'. A small intervention in the right place at the right time can ultimately move 'the whole big ship of state'. His epitaph reads 'CALL ME TRIMTAB'.

When Katrina and I set up an entity to channel our philanthropy, we named it the Trimtab Foundation. We don't mind going first, or taking reasonable risks with our philanthropy, but we're always looking for ways in which our giving might catalyse change in orders of magnitude greater than we could ever achieve on our own.

STRIKING AT THE ROOT

In mid-2018 I caught up with Mariam Alsikafi, one of the first friends I'd made in my freshman year at college in the United States two decades earlier. Mariam had gone on to Harvard and her class had built the Leadership Now Project, a non-profit focusing on specific issues undermining US democracy.

Mariam's story jogged my memory of a talk I'd seen by Professor Lawrence Lessig, then of Stanford, now of Harvard. Lessig made the point that the democratic process in the republic he loved, America, had been perverted by the influence of big money. He argued that without a well-functioning democracy, vested interests would hold back progress. Lessig powerfully began that 2011 talk with a line from Henry David Thoreau: 'There are a thousand hacking at the branches of evil to one who is striking at the root.' Lessig said that fixing democracy requires us to strike at the root—everything else is just hacking at the branches. Furthermore, he argued that while electoral reform might not seem the *most important* of issues, it was the *first* issue.

I learned about the political action committee (PAC) Lessig built to strike at the root. The Mayday PAC, launched on 1 May 2014, sought to raise funds to support candidates who would fight for electoral reforms. I loved his clear response to the obvious question: 'Yes, we want to spend big money to end the influence of big money … Ironic, I get it. But embrace the irony.' Mayday raised US$12 million and had mixed success, helping one congressman retain his seat and a new candidate to secure a seat in Congress, but missed out in six other races.

In the month after the Medevac vote triumph, the threads all came together: Lawrence Lessig's clarion call to strike at the root, in particular his idea to fund candidates; my friend Mariam's audacity to just do it; and my ringside seat observing the value and strength of the independents in the Australian Parliament. My experience had shown me that change from within was effectively impossible, but I could now see a pathway to fixing our broken political system. My involvement with Hepburn Wind, energy commentating and #KidsOffNauru had given me the confidence to engage with politics.

Buckminster Fuller's assertion that the individual can be a trimtab, can literally turn the ship of state around, provided the final nudge. Not only could I see that I was well placed to give it a go, I *had* to give it a go.

With the 2019 federal election looming, I explained my idea to Michael Bradley and Kiera Peacock of Marque Lawyers. I wanted to set up a fundraising entity not unlike Kooyong 200, but instead of supporting a particular candidate from a particular party, I wanted to support multiple candidates who would fight for climate and integrity. Peacock suggested a structure and I gave her the go-ahead. It needed a handle and it made perfect sense to name it Climate 200. Kerryn Phelps introduced me to Damien Hodgkinson, her campaign accountant, and I asked him to recommend a director with a good under-standing of electoral funding laws. Hodgkinson loved the whole idea and volunteered himself on the spot.

Over the six weeks between setting up the initiative and the May 2019 election, I called everyone I knew in climate philanthropy and raised $495 000 from twenty-eight donors. With the help of a volunteer, we contacted candidates we thought worthy of support and prioritised our donations according to where we thought they'd have the biggest impact. Across the climate movement, there was great optimism that this election would be the climate election, and although Climate 200 had been late on the scene, we'd hoped we'd make a difference.

The climate election wasn't to be, however. The Coalition government, with its destructive stance on climate action, was returned, to the surprise of many—not least the government itself. I was exhausted and in need of a break from politics. We worked our way through the com-pliance activities and put Climate 200 into hibernation.

PIECES COMING TOGETHER

My first substantive conversation with Byron Fay was on the margins of Al Gore's Climate Reality conference in Brisbane the month after the 2019 election. Byron had just wrapped up a stint working as an adviser to independent senator Tim Storer, seeing first-hand the positive impact independents can have on the parliament. 'Everything on its merits and no deals' was Storer's refreshing mantra.

Almost two years later, I called Byron to find he was on a surfing holiday in Costa Rica, having completed a stint at a Joe Biden–aligned PAC during the 2020 US presidential election. I told him I thought the Climate 200 model—not unlike a PAC—could work at the next Australian federal election, that I was keen to get Climate 200 up and running again, but that it needed a more sophisticated strategy and a longer runway than in 2019. I thought a warts-and-all post-mortem was a good place to start and, recalling Byron's experiences in Storer's office, it struck me that he would be the perfect person to lead it. Luckily, he agreed to getting involved.

I also believed it was critical that the review draw on the experience of a campaign veteran, someone who'd actually run and won an election campaign. ('Run and won' became a mantra at Climate 200.) I found the perfect expert in Anthony Reed, who had run Kerryn Phelps's winning campaign in the 2018 Wentworth by-election and Zali Steggall's in 2019.

The first major conclusion we reached was that, at a fundamental level, Climate 200 had worked. People had been prepared to donate to it. That money was then on-donated to candidates who were ambitious about climate and integrity, and the support had helped some of those candidates to be elected. In terms of the assistance we gave to those who won, our support of Helen Haines may have been the most strategic. Haines won by 2816 votes, a margin of 1.4 per cent. Our donation helped procure advertising on TV, digital platforms, radio and in local newspapers. While it was impossible to determine what would have happened without Climate 200's donations, given the slender margin, it seemed plausible that our contribution had made a difference.

There were also some narrow misses. Kerryn Phelps was defeated by fewer than 2400 votes in Wentworth. While we had provided Phelps with our third-largest 2019 donation ($47 500), I came to deeply regret not making a larger contribution to her campaign. In hindsight, we placed too much faith in the benefits of incumbency. The result was a reminder of how hard it was going to be for independents to hold seats when facing the might of the major party machines.

It was even harder to stomach given that several great campaigns we donated to fell flat. Father Rod Bower, for example, only received 0.6 per cent of the vote in his bid for a NSW Senate seat, teaching us that it's incredibly difficult for an independent to win a Senate seat, especially in the larger states like New South Wales and Victoria.

The broader lesson was that we should have focused our resources on a smaller number of candidates with greater potential, rather than spreading them too thinly among a wider pool. Perhaps the most important finding was the most obvious: we'd started way too late in 2019. Election campaigns need the bulk of their funding committed many months before election day, but we'd disbursed most of our funding in the final fortnight, when voters had already made up their minds and it was difficult to spend the money efficiently.

The review also identified a new factor. Community groups had emerged around the country aiming to replicate the success of McGowan and Haines in Indi, and Steggall in Warringah. Most of these groups had the word 'Voices' in their name—Voices of Goldstein, Voices of Wentworth—which some mistook as a signal they were formally aligned. It's not a franchise—there is no head office, there are no rules. In a way, they're a bit like book clubs: no-one needs permission to set one up, some are serious, some more social, some thrive, some fail. Many were being generously mentored by veterans of the Warringah and Indi campaigns. Kirsty Gold and Tina Jackson, in particular, were working with nascent but eager groups in Sydney and Melbourne. Cathy McGowan, Alana Johnson, Jill Briggs and, separately, Denis Ginnivan were helping out groups around the country, with a special focus on regional areas.

In February 2021, as the review was wrapping up, McGowan held a national convention for community independents: Getting Elected. She expected fifty people to attend and ended up with 300 from eighty-one electorates. Byron and I both attended and were blown away by the optimism, energy and openness. We also got to see the effectiveness of community organising over Zoom. It was clear that something very special was happening at the community level. Interestingly for us, action on climate and integrity seemed to be the most consistent motivators for those involved. On climate, the Black Summer bushfires and the federal government's weak response had dramatically elevated the importance of action to this nascent movement. On integrity, attendees were fired up about a spate of highly publicised rorts and pork-barrelling.

We came away from the conference thinking that the pieces were coming together: community energy, effective organising, and our plan to deliver financial support and data-driven strategic insights. I was very happy with Byron and Anthony's review and I engaged Byron to start reanimating Climate 200. I convinced another veteran from the Warringah campaign, Anna Josephson, to join Peacock and Hodgkinson on our fledgling Advisory Council. As we moved forward, I wanted a broad range of views on our council, so I was pleased that former Liberal Party leader John Hewson, former Labor Party national president Barry Jones and former Democrats leader Meg Lees also agreed to join. I managed to convince former independent MPs Kerryn Phelps, Julia Banks, Rob Oakeshott and Tony Windsor to do likewise.

From time to time I'd call Cathy McGowan for advice, and she was always generous with her time. I did ask the woman often introduced as the 'godmother' of the movement if she'd consider joining our council. After careful consideration, she gave me a warm and thoughtful rejection, explaining that she greatly valued her absolute independence, and that her Community Independents Project and Climate 200 would both be stronger if they maintained a complete separation. I'm sure she was right. Cathy offered that she was happy to speak periodically and 'swap notes', and we do to this day.

Around the same time, a wave of women's stories was engulfing the national conversation. Inspired by Grace Tame's powerful acceptance speech as the 2021 Australian of the Year, former Liberal Party staffer Brittany Higgins came forward with her own deeply disturbing story of an alleged rape in a minister's Canberra office. Not long after, the nation was shocked to hear the accusations against Christian Porter (which he strenuously denied) made by the woman known only as Kate, who took her life not long after sharing them. The prime minister verbally attacked Australia Post CEO Christine Holgate, Julia Banks published her account of ingrained misogyny in the Liberal Party, and Rachelle Miller levelled claims against a federal minister on *Four Corners*, all of which contributed to the perception that the work environment in Parliament House was toxic and unsafe for women. The Jenkins Review found that one in three Parliament House staffers had been subjected to sexual harassment at work.

The March 4 Justice rallies around the country marked a tipping point. At Climate 200, while we had fought the temptation to increase our scope from simply climate and integrity, Julia Banks convinced me to add a third value: advancing the treatment and safety of women.

HELPING TO RAISE THE DOUGH

By July, there was just one last issue to resolve: whether we should change our name. For one thing, it hid our focus on integrity and gender equity. Then there was the number 200. The idea was that we were aiming for 200 donors, but we would look terribly silly if we couldn't find them. We threw around names for a couple of days, but all the alternatives were even less inspiring. So we decided to stick with Climate 200, imperfect as it was.

We built a website with a donations portal and a fundraising slide deck. We also drew up a list of people we thought might be interested, starting with those who had donated in 2019. One of the challenges was that no candidates had yet been identified, so we were selling donors the promise of what we hoped would materialise. But we had stayed in touch with many of the community groups we'd met at Getting Elected. Most were building their campaigns: holding regular events, growing their membership, putting out feelers for potential candidates. Some had started fundraising money and developing campaign plans.

In August, with our website ready to take donations, I launched our crowdfunder with a long thread on Twitter. We received 211 donations in the first twenty-four hours. So much for being worried about not reaching 200 donors!

Within days of the new website going live, one of our early supporters, Simon Monk, took to Twitter to lay down a challenge. He would donate $100 000 to Climate 200 if 100 other people donated $1000 each. Monk's tweet somewhat caught us off guard—as did the many $1000 donations that rushed into our bank account. That was the start of an extremely successful series of fundraising matching challenges run by donors.

We also engaged Canberra press gallery veteran Jim Middleton to help us spread the word about our audacious plan. The media interest was high, and we saw a strong correlation emerge between news articles (good and bad) and donations. Before we knew it, we'd raised $2 million from over 2000 donors. We could see that we were going to easily exceed our initial target of $3 million, well before the election.

In 1996, former Victorian premier Joan Kirner established EMILY's List Australia to support progressive Labor women candidates. EMILY is not a person but an acronym, borrowed from a similar organisation in the United States, for the words 'Early money is like yeast'. This is the first part of a political saying that concludes with 'because it helps to raise the dough'. The importance of early money was twofold for Climate 200. Early money from donors helped us demonstrate momentum and 'crowd in' more donations. And early money funnelled to campaigns helped them build the momentum that was critical for bringing in more volunteers and donors.

Given the success of the Monk matching challenge, we decided to use the technique ourselves. We ran a rolling series of challenges, with larger donors only agreeing to donate a certain sum if the public matched their pledge, dollar for dollar. First up were Simon and Anna Hackett who, like Simon Monk, stumped up $100 000. The Hacketts engaged their network, I shot out some tweets, we emailed our small but growing list, and we landed a news article. Within forty-eight hours, the campaign was complete and more than $200 000 had been raised.

Then things really took off. We ran smaller but still significant campaigns, like Archibald Prize finalist Angus McDonald's $15 000 matching challenge, all the way up to a $500 000 challenge with the Milgrom family. Communities came together, too, like the group of 100 Canberrans who raised nearly $50 000 to pool into their own 'Canberra 4 Climate 200' matching campaign. And in the final days of the effort, one donor offered to add $100 to any public donation of any amount.

The larger donors loved matching challenges because they could see their contributions bringing in others. The smaller donors loved them because they could see their donations being doubled. It was a win-win situation.

Our offline strategy would have looked pretty familiar to anyone who has been involved in professional fundraising. Start with your network and pitch for a donation. Ask any donors if they have friends, relatives or colleagues who might be interested in a pitch. Likewise, identify communities of interest—for example, Australian Parents for Climate Action—and pitch to them. And recognise that if someone makes a significant donation out of the blue, chances are it'll be their first, not their last. We met with many hundreds of potential donors at more than sixty pitches over a nine-month period.

Both online and offline, several things stood out. Most of our donors had never donated to a political campaign before. Also, most wanted nothing to do with the major parties. In addition, for many there was an 'ick factor' in speaking with a politician or a political party about a donation. Donors said it felt 'cleaner' and 'more ethical' to donate through Climate 200, staying right away from the transactional cash-for-access model endemic to Australian politics.

Our fundraising ruffled feathers. When *Sydney Morning Herald* columnist Peter FitzSimons revealed that we'd raised $1.4 million in donations, Liberal Party Federal Director Andrew Hirst sent an outraged email appeal for donations to his members. We in turn launched our own fundraising appeal directly quoting Hirst's email.

In November 2021, a donor messaged me to say he had received a call from Josh Frydenberg after a donation he'd made to Climate 200 had been publicised. It was the third such call I'd heard of, and I thought it was pathetic. Frydenberg had a history of making phone calls that many would deem inappropriate, to journalists and photographers, to the directors of AGL. When Oliver Yates announced his candidacy against Frydenberg in 2019, he was immediately 'let go' by his employer Macquarie Bank, presumably due to pressure, explicit or implied. Anyway, I sent out a tweet chiding the treasurer for taking time out of his busy schedule to harass donors.

Later that afternoon I missed a call from another donor. When I finally saw the attempted contact, my heart sank—while I'd been careful not to reveal any donor's identity in the tweet, of course Frydenberg would have had a short list of who it could be. I called the donor to apologise for telling the story without his permission. Thankfully he was in a good mood. It turned out that Frydenberg had called him again, within ninety minutes of my tweet, to complain about the donor telling me about Frydenberg's first call. I'm still surprised that the treasurer of the Commonwealth of Australia had the time and inclination to make one such call, but stunned that he so quickly was alerted to my tweet and then dropped everything to call the donor a second time!

It was bloody hard work, a rolling series of online campaigns and offline pitches, but by election day we had raised $13 million from 11 200 donors. Lazy media liked to portray Climate 200's war chest as if it was my money, but while my family's donation was significant, it represented less than 2 per cent of the funds raised.

LEVELLING THE PLAYING FIELD

In the lead-up to the 2019 election, I got to know a candidate running against a particularly bad MP, an MP whose name was associated with numerous scandals and who had a reputation for fighting against climate action, not using good arguments but by wielding mistruths and through maladministration. The opposing candidate was whip-smart, ethical, personable and hardworking—a string of attributes that would have made her a much better local representative, and would have raised the bar in parliament. Her tilt was unlikely to be successful at the election, but if she ran a strong campaign, maybe she could put pressure on the incumbent and chip away at his margin, perhaps winning it over a couple more electoral cycles.

The candidate was from a major party and for various reasons didn't fit the criteria for Climate 200 support, but I thought her campaign was deserving of a personal donation. She disagreed, telling me: 'To be honest, your money would have more impact elsewhere.'

I was taken aback. Why would a candidate not grab an offer of financial support with both hands?

'It wouldn't be fair for you to invest more in my campaign than the party is planning to,' she said. She then explained that, as a candidate running in a seat the party considered unwinnable, she would receive a box of T-shirts, a few hundred corflute signs to put up around the electorate, and several cartons of how-to-vote cards. She wouldn't be given a single helper from head office for the campaign and therefore was her own campaign manager. The party's investment in the seat was well less than $10 000, maybe even half that.

Of course, on polling day the party's rank and file would still hand out how-to-vote cards, and the candidate was running under the party's well-established brand. In the final wash-up, she won more than 25 000 primary votes and helped bring in almost as many for the party in the Senate. In 2019, the AEC paid out $2.76 per primary vote in public funding. (Since the funding can only be paid after the final vote tallies are known, the money is only useful for paying back debts or paying for future campaigns.) So on a very modest direct investment, the party 'earned' approximately $140 000 in public funding from the particular seat I was watching. In this manner, established parties leverage their strong brands to 'harvest' healthy profits from non-priority electorates, adding to the war chests they need for future contests in target seats.

Independent campaigns don't get this benefit. Having, in most cases, no established brand, the independent candidate must build one. There are no other seats from which they can 'harvest' public funding. They receive public funding, but it arrives too late and in aggregate is dwarfed by the investment they must make to establish even the most basic name recognition.

In March 2022, Liberal donors paid $14 000 to sit next to prime minister Scott Morrison at a dinner in Perth. Trent Zimmerman raised hundreds of thousands of dollars in North Sydney by giving donors access to senior ministers at similar events. Labor in opposition also raised hundreds of thousands of dollars by promising donors access to potential future ministers. Independent challengers can't sell access to ministers, and while they can ask for donations at events, businesses are very reluctant to be seen as financing the campaign of a contender.

Members of parliament receive other benefits. Their publicly funded office staff are often deployed during campaigns to assist the member's re-election. Ministerial staff and those of senators not facing re-election are also often seen helping out. While incumbent independents can take similar advantage of publicly funded help, non-incumbent independents must fundraise for staff or find volunteers.

If you visited the Kooyong pre-poll booth on Guest Street, Hawthorn in May 2022, you'd have seen both Monique Ryan and Josh Frydenberg flanked by 15–20 helpers. At most, one of Ryan's helpers was paid; the rest were volunteers. Chances are the majority of those handing out cards for Frydenberg were on the public payroll.

The advantages don't stop there. Incumbents have an annual communications allowance of up to approximately $250 000 that is to be spent on non-electoral matters. While most MPs are careful not to overtly break the rules, every fridge magnet, piece of mail and Facebook advertisement that carries the MP's face establishes a publicly funded edge over their challengers. Chances are that just before the last election, you coincidentally received a few definitely-not-electoral-matter letters from your MP touting their achievements. Over a three-year election cycle, these communications and staffing benefits could easily total more than $1 million in publicly funded electioneering.

The first $1500 donated to a political party is tax-deductible, any day of the year. However, the same donation to an independent candidate is only deductible from the declaration of nominations, at most a month before polling day. By this point, a good campaign will have spent the majority of its funding and committed all the rest. The timing disparity confers a huge fundraising advantage on the parties.

The parties also have access to the electoral roll. This list of every voter and their address is critical to the sophisticated analysis common to modern election campaigns, to doorknocking and the sending of addressed mail. But independent challengers only gain access to the electoral roll mere weeks before an election, in its printed form. This is too late to be useful. To have the most basic information on voters at hand, independent challengers must pay for commercially available lists, which can cost upwards of $40 000 for one electorate.

Also consider that the previous federal government commissioned a $31 million ad campaign that ran right up to the day the 2022 election was called. The campaign, entitled 'Positive Energy', sought to neutralise the truthful narrative that Australia was a laggard on climate. It used claims that were closer to lies than spin to try to convince Australians—that is, voters—that the government had done a great job on emissions reduction and the shift towards renewable energy.

So when you add it up, independents need to raise hundreds of thousands of dollars and build a base of highly committed, talented and experienced volunteers before the playing field is remotely even. And that's where Climate 200 comes in. We can accelerate fundraising, through matching challenges and strategic profile building, and we can give campaign advice on how to maximise the value of limited funds and restricted volunteer numbers.

After Clive Palmer spent big at the 2019 election, there were renewed calls for donation and expenditure caps, but nothing ever happened. One of the side effects of Climate 200 raising the visibility of political donations is that such calls are once more in vogue. Countless column inches and hours of airtime have focused on the 'vast' sums of money we brought into the election. In fact, our contribution was relatively small—as stated earlier, we spent almost $13 million on the campaign. We'll likely never know exactly how much the parties spent, but we do know that in 2019 their *income* was huge: $181 million for the Coalition, $126 million for Labor, $84 million for Palmer's UAP and $20 million for the Greens. Readers may argue that the parties contest many more seats than the twenty-three we concentrated on, but most seats are not seriously challenged, and are in fact a source of income. By any measure, Climate 200 is a relative minnow.

We're all for a national discussion on levelling the electoral playing field—a key plank in restoring integrity to parliament—but to be fair, which is a requirement in a healthy democracy, the discussion needs to be broadened beyond donations. Australia deserves a root-and-branch review of electioneering that surfaces all of the advantages enjoyed by parties, incumbents and members of the government. The review needs to identify reforms that make elections fairer rather than further entrenching incumbency. Until such time, independent campaigns will require significant financial support to have a fighting chance against the incumbents and the party machines.

NO STRINGS ATTACHED

A Climate 200 donor once called to let me know he was donating $5000 to a minister's re-election campaign. I told him he didn't need to tell me about it, that it didn't concern me at all, but he wanted to tell me why. The donor explained that the $5000 would give him 'telephone rights'—that is, having made the donation, he could be sure that he had a hotline to the minister. Of course, it wasn't documented, and likely was never even spoken about, but nonetheless the tacit arrangement had been in place over several election cycles. It's no surprise to me that Australian politics can be so transactional, but I was shocked to discover that some politicians are so cheap. Apparently, three years of 'platinum support' from the Australian Government can be bought for approximately $1700 a year!

Cash for access is a corruption of our democracy. Every Australian should have equal access to our representatives, or, given that there simply aren't enough hours in a parliamentary career to spend time with every constituent, it'd be fair to mete out MPs' limited time based on constituents' needs. Access certainly shouldn't be influenced by donations.

I was determined that Climate 200 would not operate on this level. If we were no different to traditional, transactional donors, it would fly in the face of our commitment to restore integrity to politics. Engaging in quid pro quo would undermine our credibility and that of the candidates we hoped to support. Not that we had a choice—there's no way that the independents I'd met would entertain any such discussion, which for me is a large part of their appeal.

Cynics, especially from the media and the Liberal Party, find it very difficult to believe that anyone could donate to a candidate without receiving a direct personal benefit. Many are adamant that there must be some sort of contract that binds candidates in exchange for Climate 200's support. While this says a lot about their warped view of the world, it's also silly. What accountability could there be to us? We can't threaten independents with expulsion when there's no membership! And any secret agreement signed with twenty-three candidates would surely come to light and make for political dynamite.

While some might argue that it's senseless to provide significant donations without accountability, ultimately the candidates are accountable to their communities. If they're not faithful to the values they campaigned on, they won't win a second term. We didn't need to create some kind of enforceable obligation—democracy had already provided a better one.

We did produce a boring, single-page funding agreement setting out how our donations were made on an arm's-length, no favours, no strings attached basis. It began by stating our shared values, that donations may be used at the discretion of the recipient, and that Climate 200 would not seek any influence whatsoever over a candidate. It required that both parties comply with all applicable laws, and that the campaign establish a code of conduct for both the candidate and its volunteers. Candidates were required to ensure they were eligible for nomination under the dreaded section 44 of the Australian Constitution. The campaign was required to direct any surplus funds to activities consistent with the intent of the donation—that is, the candidate couldn't buy themselves a Porsche with leftover funds—and if the candidate breached any applicable laws or withdrew their candidacy, any unspent funds would be returned. All pretty standard stuff that you'd see in a philanthropic funding deed.

I was looking forward to being able to publish this simple, plain-English funding agreement on our website, to help set a new standard for transparency and integrity in political funding. But when we showed it to a few independents, they unanimously hated it: not because they objected to having a code of conduct or procedures to enhance integrity, but because having an agreement—even one that reinforced independence—would buttress the false narrative that our funding came with strings attached.

Going back to the drawing board, we created a simple eligibility checklist. Campaigns were free to do what they wanted, but we'd only support those that were aligned with our values, had their own codes of conduct for volunteers and the candidate, and had their own policies to manage surplus funds and ensure compliance with electoral laws. Once we'd determined that a campaign was eligible, it was invited to apply for funding, in bite-sized chunks. A committee evaluated each application, considering a range of metrics to determine the strength of the campaign, including its most recent polling.

It was a simple, data-driven process that ensured Climate 200 and the campaigns maintained the complete independence so fundamental to the movement.

NOT A PARTY, REALLY

Throughout the 2022 campaign, mischievous media sought to paint Climate 200 as a party, fundamentally—and sometimes wilfully—misunderstanding how we operate and our role within the community independents movement.

At every election, there's a slew of independent candidates who each receive fewer than 1000 votes. No doubt many of them are every bit as impressive (or unimpressive) as the candidates preselected for the major parties, but without strong campaigns, they're unlikely to fetch 1 per cent of the vote. Climate 200 was approached dozens of times by people who wanted us to 'run them' as an independent. We turned every single one of them down, explaining that we do not choose or run candidates or start campaigns. Rather, we support genuine local campaigns. We wait for good campaigns to emerge and, if invited, we help them scale to a win. We look at three simple measures when deciding whether or not to offer support.

Firstly, a campaign must meet our eligibility criteria, the most important of which is values alignment—we will only support campaigns that are committed to a science-based response to climate change, rooting out corruption from our political system, and advancing the treatment and safety of women. Values, not policies. We explicitly haven't defined policies, as it is up to independents to consult with experts and their communities and form their own. And frankly, there's no way that the type of independent campaigns we're looking for would accept a list of policies from a donor!

Secondly, it must be a strong campaign. That means, to begin with, a great campaign team—a mix of winners representing a range of skills and demographics. The team must include leaders and doers, communicators and community organisers. And I'm a firm believer that a campaign needs at least one person who has run and won a campaign before. Many of the 2022 campaigns were fortunate to find people in their community who had been part of winning campaigns, and a few engaged professionals such as Anthony Reed and Ed Coper of Populares. (In the lead-up to the last election, only a handful of people in the country had been close to the centre of a winning community independent campaign, but going into the 2025 election there will be well over fifty newly minted experts who have now 'run and won'.)

A strong campaign also requires a track record of running events that people actually turn up to, a strong volunteer base, and a proven ability to fundraise locally. If a federal campaign can't run a handful of events with more than 100 attendees, encourage 200 people to sign up as volunteers, and raise, say, $50 000, it probably doesn't have the social and political capital to win the 30 000 or more votes required to win at an election.

The selection of a great candidate is another key aspect of a robust campaign. The candidate doesn't have to be nationally famous, but they do need to have deep networks throughout the electorate, be smart, a great communicator, telegenic, resilient and free of scandal. Mostly, these are the qualities that the parties are looking for, but with one key difference. The parties generally recruit from a tiny pool: party members within their communities who have jostled, demonstrated and earned loyalty, and developed networks of patronage over many years. The pool of candidates that community independent campaigns draw from is much larger, though admittedly, most of the potential candidates lie somewhere between reluctant and repulsed when it comes to politics. (That is changing as the population begins to understand the difference between a crossbench MP and a major party MP.)

Finally, the campaign must have a clear path to electoral success. There's no point investing time and money if polling indicates that a seat is not in play.

Climate 200 has never started a campaign, nor chosen a candidate. Every campaign we've supported began within their community and showed us they had a head of steam before we chose to turbocharge them.

THE GOOD BLOKE ADVANTAGE

In April 2021, as we were planning our relaunch, Byron and I had a Zoom call with Ruth McGowan. Ruth is one of Cathy McGowan's nine sisters and is very actively involved in politics. She trains hundreds of women a year through the Pathways to Politics and Women for Election programs, helping women to overcome their natural hesitation to put their hands up for politics. Ruth explained to me that the main barrier is a lack of confidence. Too many accomplished women, she's found, worry that they aren't up to the challenge. She pointed out that vanishingly few men suffer from this same affliction!

Ruth set Byron and me a challenge. We've all heard certain politicians referred to as 'good blokes'. People will say, 'I don't agree with everything Barnaby says, but if you meet him, he's a good bloke.' A male politician can be deeply flawed, yet if they're considered a 'good bloke', all will be forgiven. Ruth asked us, 'So what is the female equivalent of this good bloke advantage?'

We went quiet, thinking about a response. 'Good woman' didn't sound right, plus I couldn't think of a woman who had received a leave pass because they were considered one. Twenty seconds went by and we were still drawing blanks. Ruth then said, 'Don't worry. I've been thinking about this for twenty years and there is no female equivalent of the good bloke advantage.'

Ten months later, when I briefly stepped back to write a National Press Club speech about the movement, I called Ruth to let her know I finally had an answer for her. There isn't an exact female equivalent to the good bloke advantage, but I think Australia is at a point where the crossbench has seen a string of 'no-nonsense accomplished women'—from Cathy McGowan to Rebekha Sharkie, Julia Banks to Kerryn Phelps, and from 2019, Zali Steggall and Helen Haines. You'll never see them driving a clown car for attention, mugging for the cameras while dust-mopping a gymnasium after a flood, washing a hapless customer's hair, or tackling primary school soccer kids to the ground.

The crossbench suits these women. They wouldn't put up with the typically messy snakes-and-ladders path through a party, where career progression too often depends on doing someone else's dirty work and compromising the very values that make them interesting in the first place.

Over decades, I've heard people bemoan the fact that many very talented Australians won't go near politics, leaving us with a preponderance of career politicians who started in university politics and rose through the ranks without ever holding down a job in the real world. It's been very exciting to see the crossbench become an attractive pathway for successful non-politicians to serve their communities and their country. These are the calibre of politicians we've always wanted.

RELENTLESSLY POSITIVE

As we were determined to be driven by data rather than emotion, a robust polling program was always going to be central to our efforts. Quality data would give us the confidence to make hard decisions, and offer campaigns the information they needed to run effective and efficient races. We engaged Kos Samaras at Redbridge and Valerie Bradley, a US-based polling expert, to design our program. Bradley had run Joe Biden's analytics polling program during his successful 2020 US presidential campaign, and Samaras had a long history polling for the ALP and industry groups in Victoria.

In mid-2021, we polled three electorates where we knew strong community campaigns were building: Mackellar, Wentworth and North Sydney, all bordering Steggall-held Warringah. From what we had heard, Steggall's brand was strong in those seats, so instead of just asking about a generic independent, we asked specifically about how people would vote if the independent was a candidate 'like Zali Steggall'. The results blew us away. In North Sydney, the vote for a generic independent was 16 per cent. That vote shot up to 28 per cent when it was an independent 'like Zali Steggall', which could put a candidate like that in a winning position. Similar results were obtained in the other electorates.

But, as one sceptical donor said at the time, 'Zali Steggalls don't grow on trees. She's a barrister and a four-time Olympian!' It was a fair point. But we knew there were people who would make great community inde-pendent candidates in these seats—the communities just needed to find them. We also learned that climate change was consistently a major issue for voters. It was the *most* important consideration for voters in North Sydney and Wentworth, and the second priority in Mackellar.

Our next round of polling, in Goldstein, Kooyong, Flinders and Higgins in Victoria, performed using Helen Haines as the reference point, yielded even more compelling results. (Higgins was arguably the most pro-pitious seat for an independent that we polled, but for whatever reason, no community independent campaign arose there.)

In late October, our fundraising total passed $3 mil-lion, but with only Kylea Tink announced as a candidate, a new anxiety grew. What if we raised a bunch of money and the community campaigns couldn't find candidates?

Fortunately, we didn't have to wait long. On 20 November, Wentworth Independent, a community group, announced they'd selected Allegra Spender as their candidate. Soon after, one or two candidates were being announced each week, among them Zoe Daniel in Goldstein, Monique Ryan in Kooyong and Sophie Scamps in Mackellar. By mid-December, most of the candidates had been announced by their communities and their campaigns were in full swing—there would be more than a dozen candidates by Christmas. And their primary vote numbers were creeping up from low bases of around 10 per cent. Before breaking for Christmas, we also made a number of donations enabling the independents' campaigns to advertise heavily over the following weeks, as we knew they quickly needed to build name recognition.

After a break in January, there was another wave of candidate announcements. Over February, March and April, we kept fundraising and making strategic donations to campaigns as fast as we could. Donations kept climbing. We kept polling, and with each new round we saw the primaries for the independents rising, and numbers their competitors would find deeply depressing. Then, as soon as the election was called, when 'normal people' started tuning into politics, the support for independent candidates in the most prominent seats exploded. It wasn't just their policy platforms that voters were responding to. It was also the way they were running their campaigns: relentlessly positive, inclusive, volunteer-driven, grass-roots community efforts.

It was clear that the movement was banking wins well before election day. Activists had for years been trying to stop oil and gas exploration off Sydney's northern beaches, but it wasn't until Zali Steggall and Sophie Scamps made it an election issue that Morrison intervened to kill the exploration licence. Likewise, the government bowed to pressure and restored part of the ABC's funding, and released refugees who had been detained for years in Melbourne hotels. Seasoned political observers have told me that pressure from the teals on heartland Liberal seats was a major driver of Morrison's net-zero emissions commitment. (It reminded me of how my father would position himself in deals such that whatever the outcome, he'd win either way.)

Our polling in early April showed us that if the trend we had seen emerge over the previous months held, then seven candidates we had supported were on track to win. We were further buoyed by the fact that climate change and integrity remained among the top three issues across all seats. And so it was: Chaney, Daniel, Ryan, Scamps, Spender, Tink and Pocock all won.

And that wasn't the end of it. Nicolette Boele fell just 4096 votes short of taking Bradfield in New South Wales, delivering a 15 per cent primary swing against Liberal Paul Fletcher—the largest swing at the 2022 election. Before the election, a commentator had told me it was impossible to pry Bradfield from the Liberals' grip: 'Bradfield would vote in Caligula's horse if it wore a blue tie.'

It wasn't just a city phenomenon either. In the National Party seat of Cowper on the NSW North Coast, Caz Heise came within 2.3 per cent of victory. In the rural seats of

Calare in New South Wales and Wannon in Victoria, Kate Hook and Alex Dyson made it into the final two, delivering massive blows to the National and Liberal primaries.

PARTISAN POT SHOTS

I learned first-hand that the Coalition enjoys the almost unequivocal support of News Corp as an arm of its communications and dirty tricks teams, with the media group regularly regurgitating without digestion material fed them by the fevered minds in the Coalition HQ. According to the online news site *The Shot*, Sky After Dark dished out fully 261 separate insults during the election campaign to Climate 200 and 'Voices of' community candidates, but just one compliment.

News Corp reporters and columnists regularly dubbed me a 'puppet master' and the candidates 'puppets', insulting the integrity of the accomplished professional women running for office, and the communities that had chosen them. 'So-called' and 'fake' became the modifiers of choice, slurs on the candidates' motivation and their independence. Time after time, News Corp unquestioningly recited Morrison's line that Climate 200's agenda was to 'sneak' Labor into government.

There were regular complaints that the independents were only targeting Liberal-held seats, hardly a surprise given that the Coalition had been in power for close to a decade—a decade of delay and denial of climate change, one of the community independents' top priorities.

Unsurprising, too, given that candidates were promoting integrity in politics and the advancement of gender equity at a time when the electorate rated the government very poorly on both counts.

Ironically, the hit jobs on Climate 200 and the independent candidates often worked in our favour. A front-page and double-page *Herald-Sun* spread on Monique Ryan resulted in a huge spike in donations, and our polling showed that her name recognition had been vastly improved. We'd often turn the criticisms into a fundraising appeal.

Still, the attacks were relentless, and we assumed they must have been found to be effective in Liberal focus groups. But when we commissioned our own focus groups in April 2022, composed of people who had historically voted Liberal but were considering backing an independent, we found that the attack lines weren't cutting through. Participants were aware that these professional women had given up 'high-level careers' and were 'passionate' and 'compassionate'. They found claims that the women had been put up to it as 'Labor stooges' to be simply not credible. In fact, the traditional Liberal voters saw the teal candidates as 'disenchanted Liberals … just like them … sick of the right faction of the Liberal Party'. It was a good lesson to learn: just because the opposition is firing bullets doesn't mean they're hitting a target.

News Corp tried to paint me as a bully, amplifying questionable claims from people they'd ordinarily bully themselves. One tabloid journalist wrote a story putting words into my mouth, trying to drive a wedge between me and the independent candidates. When I asked him why his paper was targeting me, he claimed that his editors thought I was 'decapitating democracy'. Pot. Kettle. Black.

The one tactic that did get my blood pressure up was the disgraceful weaponisation of confected claims of anti-Semitism for political gain. Zoe Daniel was attacked for adding her name to a 2021 letter calling for improved media coverage of Palestine, Allegra Spender because one of the founders of her campaign had retweeted posts relating to the artist-led boycott of the Sydney Festival in protest against Israeli sponsorship, and Monique Ryan because in 2017 she'd reposted a meme that mashed up Trump's incomprehensible and infamous 'Covfefe' tweet with a book cover in the style of Hitler's *Mein Kampf*. The truth is that none of the candidates have an anti-Semitic bone in their bodies. Yet the News Corp–Liberal machine thought they'd struck gold. As sure as night follows day, *The Australian* would give prominence to an article associating a teal candidate with anti-Semitism, and minutes after publication, a very threatened Tim Wilson, Dave Sharma or Jason Falinski would draw attention to it on Twitter.

The Australian tried hard to tar me with the anti-Semitic brush. On two occasions, Sharri Markson sent me a demanding list of questions with just two hours to respond. In both cases I let her know that she had the wrong end of the stick. *Sky News*, meanwhile, gave airtime to Victorian Liberal powerbroker Michael Kroger, who listed all of the alleged anti-Semitic transgressions of the independent candidates, and dragged me into it as well owing to the fact that my mother signed a pro-Palestinian petition in 2011. Kroger seemed to imply that the Climate 200 candidates were anti-Semitic because Frydenberg was Jewish, Sharma was a former ambassador to Israel and Tim Wilson had a relatively high Jewish population in his electorate. No, the accusation doesn't make sense to me either.

The nadir of the attacks on me came when Liberal campaign HQ sent John Howard to Kooyong, ostensibly to prop up Josh Frydenberg's campaign, and I put out the following tweet:

> May 17, 2022
> @LiberalAus's 'angel of death'—john howard—is expected at #KooyongVotes prepoll any moment.
> keep in mind he:
> - undermined kyoto agreement with the australia clause
> - then refused to ratify kyoto
> - lost the 2007 climate election _&_ his own seat.
> welcome to kooyong john!

I was referring to a description of Howard given by an unnamed Liberal to Karen Middleton for an article in *The Saturday Paper* ten days earlier: 'I look at John Howard as the angel of death. You don't send John Howard somewhere you don't need him.'

The next morning, Ray Hadley accused me of anti-Semitism on 2GB. Literally one minute later on

3AW, Neil Mitchell repeated the slur. They claimed I was comparing Howard to Josef Mengele, the infamous doctor at Auschwitz who'd carried out the most appalling 'experiments' on prisoners. Mengele is in fact one of many figures from history, religion and culture—*Wikipedia* lists fifty-seven—who have been referred to as the 'Angel of Death'. Neither I, nor I presume the Liberal who associated the moniker with Howard, were using it to refer to Mengele. Rather, I believe the reference is closer to the biblical Angel of Death from Exodus, a figure prominent in the story of Passover. This original Angel of Death has been passed down through culture over millennia and is the inspiration for the grim reaper, the spirit who appears in order to take the dying into the next world.

Just over an hour after Hadley and Mitchell had their say, James Morrow published a *Telegraph* piece repeating their claims, and saying I'd been approached for comment, yet it would be another six minutes before Morrow would leave a message on my phone, asking for a response. Like clockwork, nine minutes after that, Dave Sharma tweeted Morrow's article, dripping with confected disgust. It was almost like he knew the article was coming!

The Daily Mail went the furthest, publishing an article with the ridiculous title 'Multi-Millionaire Puppet Master of Wealthy Independents Attempting to Tear Down the Liberal Party Denies Comparing Popular Ex-PM John Howard to NAZI DOCTOR Who Tortured Jews—after Being Slammed by Aussie Holocaust Survivors'. The thought never crossed my mind, nor does that connection make any sense. As Dr Andre Oboler, CEO of the Online Hate Prevention Institute, and an expert in anti-Semitism, wrote on the news site *J-Wire* on 19 May:

> Simon Holmes à Court's comment reflected the unnamed Liberal's comment and used it in the same context. It was not a Holocaust-related comment. It was not an antisemitic comment. What we see now in the media is false claims of antisemitism, some using antisemitic tropes to present Simon Holmes à Court as some sort of Elder of Zion crossed with a Nazi. This is ridiculous. It is an abuse of the memory of the victims of the Holocaust and the Jewish community.

The thread running through all of these episodes is that, despite there being no anti-Semitism to call out, claims were confected, given hugely prominent airings in News Corp outlets, immediately tweeted by threatened incumbent Liberal MPs, and hung around for days thanks to the muppets on Sky After Dark. (My apologies to the original Muppets, who are wonderful.)

Some in the more-sensible media believed that these were precision-guided messages, targeted right into the heart of the considerable Jewish communities in Wentworth and Goldstein, aiming to 'dirty up' the challenger and reinforce the notion that only the incumbent can be trusted to stand up for the Jewish population and for Israel. I think this is too simplistic. Associating a public figure with anti-Semitism doesn't just reduce their standing among the Jewish community but also distances them from the progressives, making it a convenient but abhorrent political device—one that Dave Sharma seemingly had no qualms in using.[5]

More importantly, the manufacture of false anti-Semitic claims and their deployment for political gain cheapens the memory of the historical atrocities committed against the Jewish people, and it lessens the power of calling out real and dangerous anti-Semitism, which is, sadly, on the rise in Australia. Oboler writes:

> There are real neo-Nazis and real work that must be done to tackle them. It happens in civil society on a shoestring budget and out of the limelight. Can politicians and the media please start using their influence for good, rather than for harm?

During the election campaign, Howard visited six electorates to lend support to candidates in precarious positions. Five of the candidates lost their seats. Will the Liberal campaign HQ send Howard into the field in 2025, or will the powers that be come to understand that he's the political equivalent of the grim reaper?

THE DISRUPTERS

I cut my tech teeth in Silicon Valley, the stretch of office parks full of engineers and venture capitalists between San Francisco and San Jose which has been the source of much innovation. Silicon Valley is the home of Intel, Apple, Oracle, Netscape, Google, Tesla, Facebook, eBay, PayPal, Hewlett-Packard, Netflix, Twitter and a zillion other high-tech enterprises. It's the birthplace of the commercial internet, the cradle of dotcom. Here, there's a pervasive understanding of disruption, that the businesses of today that 'own' a market segment are highly vulnerable to upstarts harnessing new technology, new business models, clever capital, and smart, audacious, high-performing teams. When the upstarts execute well, and importantly, when they get the timing right, they can rapidly gain market share, reshaping a market segment and leaving the former behemoths greatly diminished and wondering what just happened.

Of course, disruption predates Silicon Valley. It's a process that emerges whenever there's innovation—technological, commercial, social or cultural. It has no doubt been a feature of society from the moment humans started making and trading. In recent decades, we've seen disruption of the music and film industries, the news media, the taxi industry and retailing, to name just a few. What we just saw in Australian politics was classic disruption.

Clayton Christensen discusses disruption in his 1997 bestseller *The Innovator's Dilemma*. One of his famous examples are the US steel mills. In the 1960s, the industry was dominated by a handful of integrated steel mills, complex behemoths that started with iron ore and coal and produced every type of steel product under the sun.

Then a new type of business emerged, the 'mini-mill', which produced a small subset of products with much simpler and less capital-intensive businesses. The integrated mills ceded market segments, one by one, to focus on the higher end of the market, where they believed they had an advantage. Within a couple of decades, only one integrated mill was left.

Australia's major political parties are behemoths. They each comprise an organisational pyramid that spans the federal, state, divisional, branch, local government and university levels. Their people move up through this structure, forming a pool of potential candidates for election. The parties are expert at fundraising, policy development, advertising, electioneering and political strategy. Their processes are battle-hardened, and the symbiotic relationships with the media and business they enjoy have embedded them so deeply in our society that we can't imagine government without them, even though they're not even contemplated in the Constitution. The two major parties—let's consider the Coalition as a single party here—have collectively held a tight grip on Australia for three-quarters of a century. All of which means they are ripe for disruption.

The community independents, the teals, are not the first disrupters. Notably, the Greens and the Democrats, and to a lesser degree One Nation and Palmer's UAP, have played a significant role in relaxing the hegemony of the two majors. But none has had the stunning success in the Lower House as have the independents in recent elections. Throughout the 2022 election campaign, the Coalition and their media buddies falsely characterised the community independents and Climate 200 as a party in disguise. It's normal for the dominant players to fail to recognise and understand their disrupters before it's too late, and this played to the movement's advantage.

It's not too much of a stretch to think of *each* independent campaign as a micro-party. They still need to do *most* of the things the major political parties do: find a candidate, develop policy, fundraise, and win hearts and minds during an election campaign. But just as the mini-mills didn't have to do everything that the mega-mills did to take significant market share, the indies, starting with a clean sheet of paper, built lean, modern and competitive organisations.

Freed from the complexities of the multitiered parties, and not limited to a relatively small pool of potential candidates, a community campaign can use a dramatically simplified selection process that (demonstrably) chooses very fine candidates. While the NSW Liberal Party was embroiled in internecine war over preselections, community-backed independents kept up their campaigning. And as one friend who used to work for the Liberal Party told me, the candidates chosen by the community were of such a calibre that the demoralised Liberal rank-and-file would have been asking: 'Why can't we have candidates like them?'

Major party MPs need to keep one hand free to fight internal battles, within their factions and party rooms, and dedicate significant time to shoring up their political capital, if they want to retain preselection, secure a place in Cabinet, or—for the most ambitious—have the numbers when the crucial party-room vote eventually comes. Community independents are not subjected to this massive drain on their time, energy and emotions, and can instead focus on winning campaigns and then serving their communities.

As they're not going be the party of government, community independents also don't need a policy for every single issue. They do need some policies, though, and they, much more than the MPs they're up against, need to broadcast their values and let voters know how they'll make their decisions. (And they're very capable of complex and quality policy formation when the circumstances call for it, as Zali Steggall and Helen Haines showed with their respective climate and integrity bills.)

New technology and external social forces often play a significant role in catalysing disruption, and this was very much the case in the lead-up to the 2022 election. While COVID-19 locked us into our homes and cut normal social interactions for the better part of two years, it also normalised video-conferencing, creating opportunities for new connections and ways of relating. Before the pandemic, only academics and some business types regularly attended webinars and teleconferences. By May 2020, many millions had used Zoom to attend work meetings, school and lectures, and to catch up with friends and family. One of my daughters continued tap-dancing classes via Zoom throughout the lockdowns in Melbourne.

Politics is necessarily about organising people. While parties have expended inordinate energy over decades to lure members to dull branch meetings in community halls, the 'Voices of' and emerging community independent groups have used Zoom and social media to run engaging events that rapidly built their memberships. It seemed like there was at least one online community forum taking place most nights in 2021, with attendees often preparing or eating dinner while they participated.

Decades ago, it was extremely difficult to mount a credible political campaign without the heft and sophistication of a political party. But as millions of us quickly became comfortable with remote working—video-conferencing, messaging, document-collaboration software—and with social media, online advertising and crowdfunding tools at hand, a great disruption came to political organising.

CATCHING THE WAVE

The 2022 election was a major success for Climate 200, but I often caution my team that we mustn't get ahead of ourselves. We caught a wave. That said, we were pretty sure the wave would be there, and instead of just standing on the shore, watching, we built a really good surfboard and we put ourselves in the water at the right place, at the right time, paddling at the right speed, just as that

SIMON HOLMES À COURT

perfect wave came in. And we rode it right into shore with barely a fault.

And we weren't alone. Cathy McGowan and her Community Independents Project were right there on the wave, doing their thing. And about thirty strong independent campaigns were there, too. All four of the incumbents—Helen Haines, Zali Steggall, Rebekha Sharkie and Andrew Wilkie—made it to the shore. So did another seven community independent campaigns we supported—Kate, Monique, Zoe, Allegra, Kylea, Sophie and David. Dai Le caught the wave and made it in without our support. Many more, including twelve others we supported, gave it a great shot and almost brought it home, with community independents making six additional seats marginal, or coming second after preferences.

Oliver Yates's 2019 campaign in Kooyong was thrown off track when the Greens replaced their preselected candidate with high-profile barrister Julian Burnside. Yates won 9 per cent of the vote, mostly wresting it from Josh Frydenberg in the second-biggest swing against a sitting Liberal that year, second only to Tony Abbott. When Monique Ryan announced her candidacy in December 2021, she started with 600 volunteers from Yates's campaign and a community that had only recently been introduced to the independent option.

With the dramatically increased national profile of independents, and vastly more experience under their belts, many of the communities whose candidates caught the wave but didn't quite make it have positioned themselves well for an independent win at the next federal election.

The Liberal Party has suffered the most serious blow in its history, not just from the independents but from Labor and the Greens as well. In a Sydney Institute speech, *The Australian*'s Paul Kelly said, 'I don't think there's ever been an election like this in my time as a working political journalist,' adding: 'There is now an existential issue here for the Liberals.' The party lost most of its best performers—though the standard was low—and is deeply divided over how to proceed.

Some of the Liberal Party's friends say it lost because it lacked product differentiation from Labor, while others say it lost because it stopped listening to the electorate. The rot started decades ago, when John Howard drove out half the moderates and made crossing the floor almost as rare as in the Labor Party; Abbott and Morrison then drove out the remainder. Robert Menzies wouldn't recognise the party. The 'broad church' that gave the party the numbers to hold power for two-thirds of the postwar period was broadened further and further to accommodate extremists, and the foundation under the wall closest to middle Australia was undermined. It's no surprise their church is on the edge of collapse.

Peter Dutton wouldn't be most people's first choice to mediate the reconciliation and reinvention of the party, but he's there for two reasons. Firstly, the party is so diminished that there's basically no-one else to lead, and secondly, as one senior journalist put it to me, sometimes parties need to put their most ambitious member into the top job just to let them burn out.

Labor did well at the election, building from sixty-eight to seventy-seven seats, but that's only a two-seat majority. Labor beat the Greens in Macnamara by just 594 votes, and the trend will give Josh Burns, the capable local member, many sleepless nights if Labor doesn't deliver on its climate promises. Likewise, Labor holds Gilmore by just 373 votes.

Liberal Party sources tell me that Josh Frydenberg's amateurish and ultimately unsuccessful 'Keep Josh' campaign cost upwards of $3 million and chewed up a disproportionate share of campaign staffers, trying to compete with Monique Ryan's 'sea of teal' volunteers. Labor won two seats either side of Kooyong—Chisholm and Higgins—that might not have fallen if Liberal resources had been deployed more strategically.

The electoral landscape has been changing for a long time, with both major parties seeing a general decline in their proportion of primary votes. In 2022, the Coalition won 35.7 per cent of the primary vote, their lowest level ever. Labor won just 32.6 per cent, its lowest since the days immediately after Federation. Independents and the minor parties collectively won 31.7 per cent of the primary vote. The two-party stranglehold on Australian elections has been well and truly loosened.

The Greens finally delivered on their long-held promise to increase their parliamentary representation, going from one to four seats. And they are no longer chipping away at just the Labor Party—two of the three seats the Greens picked up in Queensland came from the Liberal National Party.

The Lower House now includes sixteen crossbenchers, equal to the size of the National Party's team. The public and the media are clearly intrigued, even excited, about the possibilities. At the community level, there is a palpable sense of a democratic revival. For the community independent movement has taken much of the dirt out of politics. Climate 200 put together 11 200 donors spanning every electorate in Australia. At the local level, many noted that the movement made democracy fun. Across the twenty-three campaigns we supported, 19 000 people volunteered their time to knock on 166 000 doors and make 63 000 peer-to-peer phone calls. Volunteers loved it, they loved the results, and they're itching for more.

Anthony Reed once told me that party branch meetings were frequented by the ambitious and the lonely. The community campaigns were full of the fun-loving and the passionate.

WHERE IT STARTS AND ENDS

Back inside the Auburn on election night, the hundreds of Monique Ryan supporters, most of whom had never campaigned before, were tasting success. The ineptitude, corruption and deep unpopularity of the previous government had proven too much—if Morrison had been an effective leader and listened to the electorate, I have no doubt there'd be fewer teals in parliament today. Instead, a record number of independents now sit in parliament, beacons for other communities inspired to build their own campaigns.

After the 2019 election, we'd put Climate 200 into hibernation until almost a year before the next election, and we had no full-time staff until seven months before the poll. In the wake of the 2022 election, we've decided to retain a very capable team to make the most of the opportunities ahead. Communities feel emboldened by the recent success of the independents to have a run at the state elections, and we're working out how we can help.

We want to help ensure that community campaigns have the resources to be competitive, that they get the fundraising support, training and research needed to have a fighting chance against the majors. We're going to invest great effort in addressing the obstacles that make it less likely that community campaigns take root in some areas, and think carefully about the role we can play to increase the diversity of the movement—though the path here is not yet clear to me, given that each community selects its candidates with no regard to what's happening elsewhere. I do recognise that the patriarchy and inequality are still dominant, putting full political participation beyond the reach of many, especially women. Climate 200 still has much to do to help dismantle these barriers.

We'll keep working to level the playing field, but the success of the community independents at the next federal election will depend on the wave at the time. It will be a different wave, shaped by the Albanese government, the Dutton (perhaps) Opposition, the path blazed by the new crossbench, and, as former UK prime minister Harold Macmillan famously said, 'Events, dear boy, events.'

Australia's two-party system has largely comprised a complex, symbiotic relationship between the Coalition and Labor, with historical incursions by the Democrats and, more recently, the Greens. The election of community independents to the House of Representatives crossbench at the 2022 election came as a surprise to many, and we can surely expect an immune system response from the political ecosystem. For example, Prime Minister Albanese's changes to parliamentary staffing allocation for crossbenchers—reducing the number from four to one—could be seen as a move to limit the effectiveness of the crossbench, ensuring it doesn't become too effective, too powerful. No doubt there'll be other strategic and bipartisan attempts to clip the movement's wings.

Meanwhile, I reckon the teal movement helped Australia dodge a bullet. We saw the damage done to America and the UK by populist, post-truth leaders, and we got more than a taste of it ourselves. The 2022 election was a clear repudiation of that pathway. This leaves the Liberal Party in a very uncertain position. So far, it doesn't seem to have learnt any lessons, with Scott Morrison's assessment of his loss explained as 'sometimes people just want to change the curtains', and his party striking the same poses on climate that cost them at least nine seats— seats they have to win back if they want to govern again.

For years, we've bemoaned the fact that our parliament is full of career politicians and that our finest citizens have eschewed politics. I am finishing this book at the end of the first sitting week of the forty-seventh parliament. Four teal MPs have just given their first speeches, with the remainder to come in the following week. The speeches were magnificent. They will leave any fair-minded listener excited about the qualities and purposefulness of the teals.

Of course, the ultimate success of the community independents—whether the teals are a moment or a movement—will come down to the communities, the very place where the wave begins and ends.

ACKNOWLEDGEMENTS

Dedicated to Katrina, Will, Allegra, Acorn and Stella, who keep me grounded, connected and sane.

And to the memory of Vida Goldstein, the first woman to stand for a national parliament in the English-speaking world. Vida ran five times, unsuccessfully, always as an independent. In 2022, Zoe Daniel became the first woman, the first independent and the first centrist to be elected to the seat named in Vida's honour.

~

My journey, Climate 200 and this book owe so much to so many people with skills, integrity and generosity who appeared at just the right times. I'm deeply indebted:

To Byron and the team he assembled at Climate 200, the best I've ever worked with. To Jim Middleton, who helped me navigate the big end of media town and taught me when it was best to bite my tongue. To Anthony Reed,

Ed Coper and Kos Samaras, who gave me so much of their time and skills, and patiently answered the dumb questions of this political novice. To Julia Banks, who helped me to better understand parliament's 'women problem' and gave me moral support through the tougher moments. To Sam, Jeff, Cam, Mike, Annie, Charlie, Scott, Simon, Tracey, Dan, John, Wayne, Eytan, Ben, Alex, Matthew, Justin, Ralph, Oliver, Rob, Chris, Kay, Lachlan, Vanessa, Kris and David, for your assistance and sage advice on this amazing journey.

To Ronni Salt, for her brutal criticism when I get things wrong and the strongest support when I get things right. To Brami Jagen, who gave me the confidence to start writing. To my bubble on Twitter, who provide encouragement, ideas, expertise and juicy tip-offs. To Louise Adler, the no-nonsense accomplished woman who convinced me in a moment of weakness to write for this series, and to Paul Smitz, who made me appear more eloquent and kept the project on track.

To Climate 200's Advisory Council: Anna Josephson, John Hewson AM, Barry Jones AC, Meg Lees AO, Tony Windsor AM, Dr Kerryn Phelps AM, Kiera Peacock and Damien Hodgkinson—all of whom trusted me with their reputations and time when my plans were embryonic and success was a remote possibility.

To Dylan McConnell, Tim Baxter, Ross Garnaut, Malte Meinshausen and Mike Sandiford—I couldn't hope for a better climate and energy brains trust. To Prashan Paramanathan, Adam Valvasori and Jane Salmon, without whom I would have been of little use to the #KidsOffNauru project.

To Cathy McGowan, who I believe is truly the best 'retail politician' of our time, for actively inspiring a democratic revival and engaging so genuinely and powerfully with the next generation.

To every community independent candidate who ran at the election: those who were elected, those who came close, and those who claimed a beachhead for future efforts to achieve true, local representation—I am in awe of your achievements.

To the 11 200 donors and the tens of thousands who volunteer and work in the movement, from every corner of the country, from every walk of life, who shared the vision, dug deep and enabled our shared success.

And to my father, who valued integrity above all else.

During the campaign, and especially as I wrote this book, I thought deeply about the influence of many strong women on me: especially my wife Katrina, my mother Janet, my sister Cath, and my grandmothers Bern and Ethnee. And all the wise women not named above but who have offered wisdom and encouragement at critical moments: Karoline Kuti, Sue McKinnon, Daniela Rus, Taryn Lane, Loralle Slater, Sara Howard, Amanda Martin, Carolyn Ingvarson, Anna Rose, Zahava Ellenberg, Georgie Williams, Ranya Alkadamani, Ann Capling and Mrs Gray.

Thank you.

NOTES

1   John Elder, 'Ironies Abound in the Battle for Indi', *The Sydney Morning Herald*, 15 September 2013, https://www.smh.com.au/politics/federal/ironies-abound-in-the-battle-for-indi-20130914-2trtu.html

2   Royal Commission into Institutional Responses to Child Sexual Abuse, *Case Study 32: Geelong Grammar School*, 2017, https://www.childabuseroyalcommission.gov.au/case-studies/case-study-32-geelong-grammar-school

3   Mike Seccombe, 'Exclusive: Frydenberg Pushed AGL to Sack Boss', *The Saturday Paper*, no. 357, 10–16 July 2021, https://www.thesaturdaypaper.com.au/news/politics/2021/07/10/exclusive-frydenberg-pushed-agl-sack-boss/162583920012027#hrd

4   Simon Holmes à Court, 'Why Liddell Is Likely to Close in 2022, and Why You Shouldn't Care', *The Guardian*, 9 April 2018, https://www.theguardian.com/commentisfree/2018/apr/09/why-liddell-is-likely-to-close-in-2022-and-why-you-shouldnt-care

5   Paul Sakkal, 'Holmes à Court Mulling Defamation Suit against Media Outlets and Sharma over Nazi Reference', *The Age*, 18 May 2022, https://www.theage.com.au/politics/federal/holmes-a-court-mulling-defamation-suit-against-media-outlets-and-sharma-over-nazi-reference-20220518-p5ami2.html